What You Do Shows Who You Are

The 6 Marks of a Disciple of Jesus

Mike Falkenstine

What You Do Shows Who You Are: The 6 Marks of a Disciple of Jesus

Copyright 2019 by Mike Falkenstine

Published by One Eight Catalyst, P.O. Box 630336, Littleton, CO 80163

www.OneEightCatalyst.org

All rights reserved. No part of this book may be reproduced or transmitted in any form or by any means, electronic or mechanical, including photocopying, recording, or by an information storage and retrieval system - except for brief quotations in reviews or articles - without permission in writing from the publisher.

Unless otherwise noted, all Scripture quotation are from The Holy Bible, English Standard Version. ESV® Text Edition: 2016. Copyright © 2001 by Crossway Bibles, a publishing ministry of Good News Publishers.

Additional copies of this book can be found on Amazon.com

The author would be happy to communicate with you about any questions, comments or suggestions you may have. Please follow Mike on Twitter at @MissionsMike or Facebook at MissionsMike2

ISBN: 978-1-7336283-0-3

Table of Contents

Acknowledgments — 01

Foreword — 03

Introduction — 06

Chapter 1

On Becoming a Disciple — 11

Chapter 2

The First Mark of a Disciple of Jesus: Identified with Christ — 20

Chapter 3

The Second Mark of a Disciple of Jesus: Supreme Love for Jesus — 32

Chapter 4

The Third Mark of a Disciple of Jesus: Obedient to the Bible — 43

Chapter 5

The Fourth Mark of a Disciple of Jesus: Fruitful for Christ — 57

Chapter 6

The Fifth Mark of a Disciple of Jesus: Filled with Love for Others — 68

Chapter 7

The Sixth Mark of a Disciple of Jesus: 80
Deny Yourself Daily

Chapter 8

Living Life as a Disciple of Jesus 93

Resources

Extended Time Alone with God 109

Sharing Your Testimony 113

Three-Point Bible Study Guide 117

Spiritual Gifts Study 118

Sharing the Gospel through the Bridge Illustration 121

Leader's Guide 122

Acknowledgments

I have far too many people to thank and acknowledge, but I'd like to at least try to thank a few individuals who have made this book project doable:

I am thankful to God for the way that He took a very confused and unsure 17-year-old me and showed me that life could look quite different through Christ. At Young Life's Frontier Ranch in the Colorado mountains, late one Saturday night in 1986, I trusted Christ to be my Savior, and turned my life over to Jesus. To say that my life was radically transformed is a gross understatement. Praise God from whom all blessings flow!

I want to thank my wife Sherie, who is the most wonderful person I know. To love me and tolerate me through my ups and downs means everything to me. Sherie, this book is possible because you have stood through a lot and I am thankful for you. I love you and I thank God for bringing you into my life!

My three children are some of the best people I know, and I am thankful for each of you and the way that you make my life better.

Sarah Elizabeth, you are becoming such a great woman of God and I can't wait to see what God does in and through your life and career in Music Education.

Isaac, what can I say? I was only given one chance to raise a son, and I am very proud of the man you are becoming. I pray that God would use you in mighty ways.

Anna, as the youngest, you are kind, patient and as I like to say, 'one cool customer.' There is not much that shakes you and I am thankful for the way God made you.

In 1991, I was still an unsure young man with no job prospects and no real direction outside of my emerging faith in Jesus. W. Brad Miller of the Navigators began meeting with me weekly, and God used our times together to change the course of my life. Anyone who does not believe in the power of one-on-one discipleship is wrong—I am living proof! Thank you, Brad, for your impact on my life. Everything God has used me to accomplish, from the 300,000 Chinese who have accepted Christ though our ministry to book projects like this book are possible because you stepped up and invested the time in me that I needed. I will be forever grateful and cannot imagine what my life would be today had God not led you to step in and show me that God could father me in ways that my earthly father could not. I praise God for you!

In 2008, when I wrote the first edition of the Chinese Puzzle, Tricia Lott Williford was my book editor. Tricia has gone on to become a successful author in her own right, and when it came time for the editing of this book, Tricia recommended her mother, Polly Lott. Polly, thank you for your diligent, excellent work and I look forward to working together on future book projects!

Finally, I am thankful for Todd Wagner, who wrote the foreword for this book and is the Senior Pastor of Watermark Community Church in Dallas. This church is an example of how a church really can take the Bible and use it as a complete guide for biblical church. Todd, I am very thankful for the way God is using you and your church, and I want you to know that God has used your example to bring about a resurgence of my belief that God is still working in the church today. Thank you for your contribution to this book, and I look forward to seeing how God will continue to use you and your Watermark team for the advancement of His kingdom.

Foreword

I have heard it said that if you get one good illustration or transforming idea from a book that it was worth its price, and I am pleased to tell you that if that axiom holds true you won't need to get past page 10 to feel good about your purchase of this book. Waiting for you there is one of my all-time favorite illustrations to use about the foolishness of man and the hard heartedness that subverts our way. I won't ruin the illustration waiting for you there but let me encourage you to keep reading so you don't run into trouble of your own because you failed to yield to the clear encouragement of the Scriptures to follow Jesus in all things.

In *What You Do Shows Who You Are*, you will get much more than a sobering illustration that the "sin which so easily entangles us" is not an information problem. Throughout the book you will get winsome and biblical encouragement that will help you *apply* the information God has clearly provided for us in His Word so that we don't crash into the futility of a squandered life.

Our world is constantly pulling us toward all kinds of activities that are less than best for our souls and ultimately tragic for the souls entrusted to us. But God's kindness woos us back to intimacy with him and then unleashes us to a life of usefulness to others. There is no greater evidence of a life well lived than having dozens of lives left behind to multiply your legacy and increase the glory given to the very thing (or One) you lived for. If our success is determined by our successor then being committed to the subject matter of this book will set you up for great gladness on the day you stand to give an account.

Being the father of six and the pastor of a growing church, I am often asked if I can share some thoughts about intentionally reproducing myself in the next generation. Whether I am talking about my biological or spiritual heritage I always respond with the same way.

Have a plan. Passionately follow after Christ. Be Present.

This book will help you with the first two of those "p's" leaving you only needing to follow the example of Christ to intentionally call others to "be with you"[1] to finish the job. I am praying your time in these pages increases your ability to join with Paul in saying, "Having so fond an affection for you, we were well-pleased to impart to you not only the gospel of God but also our own lives, because you had become very dear to us."[2]

The only plan you need to effectively impact the next generation is to make a commitment to be present in the lives of others you love while you have on your heart what is on the heart of God. If you "*do that*", you will soon "*show that what you are*" is a faithful disciple and disciple maker.

I often make the observation that people say what they think, but they do what they believe. Our world has long suffered because too many people who say they think Jesus is worth following have failed to follow His example in reproducing themselves in others. I am glad you are picking up this book so that you can be encouraged to reverse the long-held tradition of Pharisees everywhere who "honor Him with their lips but their hearts are far from Him."[3]

When I and a small group of friends started Watermark in Dallas almost two decades ago, we did not want to follow in the tradition we were seeing in churches around us of those who gave lip service in many areas of church leadership, so we determined to measure our success only by our ability to be and make disciples. We were not interested in attracting large numbers. We were passionate instead about being numbered among those the King found faithful. Your interest in this book suggests the kindness of God has embedded that same desire in you. Right now, in your town where you live, there are men and woman looking for faithful Christ followers like you who will faithfully invest in them. For too long we had seen churches and ministries measure their success with unreliable signs of God's blessings. Seductive things like increased crowds, social media likes, increased podcast listeners, impressive facilities and more invitations to speak have for far too long replaced Christ-like mission. Too many church leaders have been smitten with size and need to begin preparing themselves for judgment.[4]

I am reminded of 19th century Pastor John Brown, who sent his student who had just been ordained to oversee a small congregation a note which said, "*I know the vanity of your heart, and that you will feel mortified that your congregation is very small, in comparison with those of your brethren around you; but assure yourself on the*

---

1. Mark 3:14
2. Thessalonians 2:8
3. Matt 15:8

word of an old man, that when you come to give an account of them to the Lord Christ, at his judgment-seat you will think you have had enough."

May all the marks of a disciple be increasingly yours and may your greatest joy be found in marking the lives of others that you will be ready to give an account when you stand before the King.

>
> 2 Timothy 2:2,
>
> Todd Wagner
>
> Watermark Community Church - Dallas, Texas
>
> Author of *Come and See*

---

4. Hebrews 13:17

Introduction

In Durham, North Carolina, there stands an interesting bridge. Located on the north end of town, it was built in 1923 as a railroad trestle bridge, meant to safely carry trains above the road below. In its 70-year history, this bridge has developed a very interesting claim to fame. Better known as "the 11-foot 8-inch bridge," it's very low clearance presents a challenging problem for certain vehicles that try to drive beneath it--particularly the taller vans, trucks and RV's. As these taller vehicles approach the bridge, they find difficulty in judging the low clearance of the bridge and often end up hitting the bridge with their taller vehicles. In fact, back in 2008, a local man who had taken office space across the street from this bridge began to notice the number of tall vehicles hitting the bridge, and he set up a webcam to record these collisions! His video collection of these collisions can be found on his website![1]

Over the years, the city of Durham has tried several measures to protect the bridge. First, they tried putting in a steel crash beam at the same height as the bridge, so that vehicles taller than 11 feet and 8 inches would first hit the beam and not the bridge itself. That seemed like a good plan, but over-height vehicles continued to hit the beam on a fairly regular basis (and these crashes can all be seen on the website!).

After a few years of vehicles still regularly hitting the beam, the City of Durham installed additional safety measures. Their next attempt was to install bright flashing lights that would only flash if an overheight vehicle was coming toward the bridge.

---

1 www.11foot8.com (Retrieved 2018, Dec 19.) copyright Jurgen Henn-11foot8.com

These lights are triggered by a laser beam located down the road from the bridge and can sense if a vehicle is over height. Even with these measures, drivers continued hitting the bridge on a regular basis!

Perplexed about what to do next, City of Durham traffic engineers decided to take additional measures. Today, if you approach the bridge in an overheight vehicle, not only would you see the flashing light triggered by laser, but additionally there is an overhead sign that lights up and flashes, *'Vehicle is Overheight!'* and a traffic light quickly goes from yellow to red before the vehicle can reach the bridge. While waiting at that stop light, the driver sees another illuminated sign that states, *'Your vehicle is overheight. You must turn left or right here.'* You probably know what is coming next: Yep, even still, some over-height vehicles HIT that bridge!

An even more interesting piece of this story is the amount of additional measures and training that go into ensuring that the railroad bridge is kept safe. When a driver rents a moving van in Durham, he or she must sign that a form that states they have been informed about the 11-foot 8-inch bridge! If your job involves driving a vehicle that is over 11 foot 8 inches tall, additional training is provided by your employer on routes that can be taken to avoid the bridge. And yet, the webcam still records about 18 collisions with the crash beam *every year!*

I have asked myself and a handful of friends this valid question: 'Why do people continue to hit this crash beam?' They have all the information about the bridge and the beam itself, and they can see the additional measures the city of Durham has taken to ensure that their vehicles and the bridge remain safe. And yet, the answer to this question seems to be that drivers of these vehicles continue to tell themselves, "Nah, none of this applies to me. I can make it under that bridge!"

The Western Church—a term widely used to refer to the Christ-followers in North America and across Europe --seems to think and act a lot like those who try to drive under the 11-foot 8-inch bridge. We too have all the information we need on how to live our lives for Christ through God's Word and the saturation of biblical teaching we see all around us. And yet, especially as it relates to the command of the Great Commission and the obedience God requires of that command, far too many of us are like drivers who hit the bridge: we have the information we need, but we choose to ignore it.

In my over twenty years of full-time ministry, the deep desire of my heart has been to train western Christians to make every day a missions opportunity. I believe that the Great Commission—Jesus' command to proclaim the Gospel[2], make disciples[3] and be His witnesses in local areas and around the world[4]—is a directive to all believers everywhere. On my podcast called The Made for Missions Podcast, I have interviewed many pastors, seminary professors, and other ministry leaders, asking each of them the same question: *'Do you believe that the Great Commission is a 'normal' command for all Christians?'* By asking the question, I am trying hard to find someone who will tell me *'Mike, I believe that the Great Commission command was given only for those who were within earshot when Jesus spoke the words.'* Here are a few examples of answers I've gotten on the podcast[5]:

- "The repetition and the urgency of his words both suggest that there is something really significant going on here…. Jesus gave this command to a bunch of nobodies, to go take the Gospel to all the nations and that command stands for all of us today." -Chuck Lawless, Dean of Graduate Studies, Southeastern Seminary[6]

- "The truth is that all Christians have this calling on their lives…. Absolutely, the Great Commission is a normative command given to all Christians who are serious about their faith." … -Todd Wagner, Senior Pastor, Watermark Community Church, Dallas, TX[7]

- "Short answer: yes. The Great Commission command is no different than the other commands Jesus gave during his time, and we believe they apply to our lives. So yes, the Great Commission command is very applicable to Christians lives today." – Justin Long, missions researcher, *ActBeyond*.[8]

I cannot find one ministry leader of any ilk who would give me a different answer regarding this command—all agree that it still applies today and to all of us as believers. And yet, how many of us are really making disciples in our day-to-day lives?

In this way we are much like those who keep trying to drive under the 11-foot 8-inch bridge! We have all the information we need about the Great Commission, but so few of us know how to obey this command Jesus gave us. I have invested much time over the last ten years of my life to ask this question: "Why?"

Why do most of us seem to not know what the Great Commission is and how it applies to our lives? The answer to that question is a complicated one. On one hand, fewer pastors are preaching about the Great Commission as a "normal" command

---

2. Mark 16:15
3. Matthew 28:19-20
4. Acts 1:8
5. All episodes of the podcast can be found at http://oneeightcatalyst.org/podcast-2
6. Episode 18 of the Made For Missions Podcast
7. Episode 26 of the Made For Missions Podcast
8. Episode 6 of the Made For Missions Podcast

for all Christians, either because they are not committed to the task themselves, or they see the task of the Great Commission as one just for missionaries, or, in many cases, they have settled for partial obedience. Todd Wagner, Senior Pastor at Watermark Community Church in Dallas has a great tongue-in-cheek statement about this: 'Many Church leaders in our churches today have made a deal with their congregation. They ask their attendees to give the church some money to keep the lights on and continue with programs that entertain, and in return the leaders don't ask much of the congregation in relation to obedience to Scripture. and together they say they are doing everything God asks of them.'[9] While Wagner is right in his assessment, this is clearly not all God has called us Christians individually to do, nor is it all that He requires of our churches!

I believe the first step to Great Commission fulfillment is churches full of people who are in love with Jesus, and who want to know Him better and become more like Him! These Christians, whom we would call disciples of Jesus, can't help but share what He has done in their lives and they want to tell anyone who will listen. These disciples are learning more about Jesus, they are growing in their walk with Him as they abide in Jesus, and they are then obeying the command in 2 Timothy 'and what you have heard from me in the presence of many witnesses entrust to faithful men, who will be able to teach others also.'[10] For us to be considered obedient to Jesus' Great Commission command for our lives, we would be regularly sharing Jesus with those in our sphere of influence, seeing some of those people trust Christ and then complete the cycle by seeing those new believers grow in their walk with Jesus to the point of being able to reproduce their lives in Christ with others who are walking through the same process.

In this stage of the conversation, usually most Christians I talk to begin get a confused look on their faces as their eyes begin to glaze over. *'Mike, you're not actually telling me that you would expect me to do all of that, are you?'*

Yes! If we are to believe that the Great Commission is a command for us all, then…yes I am. And more importantly, Jesus expects it of you as well. After expressly giving the commands of the Great Commission, Jesus then asks for our obedience. In John 14, for example, in two different verses Jesus states that 'If you love me, you will keep my commands'[11] and 'Whoever has my commands and keeps them, he is the one who loves me.'[12] So if the Great Commission is a command for all Christians, how are you doing at obeying it? And what does your obedience say about what you think of Jesus?

9, Wagner, Todd. Watermark Church Leaders Conference, 2016.
10. Timothy 2:2
11. John 14:15
12. John 14:21

Here's what I want you to understand: even if you are currently not sharing the Gospel, making disciples, or being a good witness to others about all that He has done in your life, you can begin. Many people that I counsel in this area have never been shown what obedience to this command looks like.

And therein lies the premise of this book: I believe that if you are a disciple of Jesus, meaning that you are fully surrendered to Jesus, you will not need to try very hard to make disciples yourself. As Jesus so eloquently tells us, 'Every good tree bears good fruit.'[13] So, before we worry about Great Commission fulfillment, let's learn what a disciple of Jesus is and what a disciple of Jesus does. In the Christian life, what you do shows who you are, and more specifically, who holds the number one spot in your life. If you are a disciple, you will want to share the gospel, make disciples and be His witness in your local area and around the world.

Here are a few points I'd like to draw to your attention as we begin. In this book, we will look deeper into the Six Marks I've identified as true of a disciple of Jesus.

- As you read this book, the *First Steps* section at the end of each chapter will be my thoughts on some first things you can do to find fulfillment or victory in the areas I've just written about in the chapter.
- The 'Discussion Questions' at the end of each chapter will be divided into two parts. First are three questions for you to answer on your own as a 'quick hit' opportunity to jot down some thoughts just as you've finished reading the chapter. The second part of the 'Discussion Questions' are designed for you to answer thoughtfully at home; then to discuss as points of conversation as you go through this book with a small discussion group. While you certainly could read this book by yourself, I hope that you will use this book as a study series for your Sunday School class, men's or women's study, or your small community group.

If you are a group leader, please facilitate discussion around these questions and feel free to add discussion questions of your own as you lead your group through this book. Also, I have included a leader's guide at the end of this book that will guide you as you lead your group through this study. I hope it's helpful to you!

Thank you for taking the journey of discovery with me as we look at the biblical description of a disciple of Jesus. I hope that you will grow in your walk with Jesus through this process and that you truly will see God working in and through your study of His Word. My heartfelt prayer is that if you are able to go through this book with other believers in Jesus, you all will grow closer together as you challenge each other to become disciples of Jesus.

---

13. Matthew 7:17

Chapter 1

On Becoming a Disciple

If you think back far enough, I am sure you remember the circumstances of how you came to know Jesus Christ as your Lord and Savior. Perhaps, like me, you grew up in a church and came to the point in your life where you chose to make your parent's faith your own. My wife and I are helping our own three children through this process now. Or, perhaps, you have a fantastic and awe-inspiring testimony of how God has brought you out of drugs, alcohol or abusive situations. But I would guess that for the vast majority of us, we land somewhere in between. For each of us, our story of how God took us from being without Him into a relationship with Him is always very special, and each story is a testimony of God's goodness in our lives.

I became a Christian on November 8th, 1986 as a high school senior. A friend whom I ran track with in high school invited me to a meeting of Young Life, a global parachurch youth ministry. I resisted his invitation at first, but after his persistent 'badgering,' I attended the meeting and was impressed right away with how real and authentic the people were. Soon I began to notice something different about these people. Growing up in a non-Christian home in suburban South Denver where very few of the families we knew were churchgoers, living each day without Christ seemed very normal. Sundays were just another weekend day to go skiing, biking or doing whatever else we felt like doing, so for me, hearing about Christ for the first time was so shocking. One of my first reactions was, 'Why have I never heard this before?'

The next eight months were wonderful, from that first Young Life meeting, to attending many Young Life Bible studies, asking the hard questions and learning what the Bible was and what it said about Jesus. At a Young Life camp in early November of my senior year in high school, I heard the gospel story in its entirety and reached this conclusion: either what the Bible said about who Jesus was and what Jesus did for me on the cross was 100% true, or it was the biggest lie ever! When we were given time to go out into the woods near the camp to think and pray, I became convinced that Jesus was a historical person and that He had died for my sins. At about 10PM that evening, I accepted Christ as my own Lord and Savior. My life has never been the same since!

According to the Bible, many things happened instantaneously when I received Jesus as my Savior and trusted Him as my Lord. I became a new creation,[1] I was adopted into the family of God as God's child,[2] I was "sanctified" and washed clean,[3] I was given eternal life with God,[4] and my citizenship for all eternity got a change in location![5] And this list is just a taste of all the wonderful changes that occur when we turn our lives over to Christ.

There is no question that when God sent His Son to die for us on the cross and we then accept that spectacular free gift of a new life in Christ, as John writes, 'but to all who did receive him, who believed in his name, He gave the right to become children of God.'[6] Indeed, we were dead in our trespasses (sins), yet through forgiveness He made us alive together with Him.[7] We know that Jesus's free gift is available to all, and when we choose to believe in Him and receive Him as Lord and Savior, 'whoever believes in him is not condemned, but whoever does not believe is condemned already, because he has not believed in the name of the only Son of God.'[8] Praise God from whom all blessings flow!

Fortunately for us all, that's not the end of story of our lives in Jesus. He never intended for us to receive Him as Savior, then go back to whatever we were doing in our own pursuits. Jesus wants us to be imitators of Him, to learn from Him and to follow Him. He wants us to be His disciples. What is a disciple?

A common definition of a disciple is someone who adheres to the teachings of another. A disciple is a student. He or she is a follower or a learner. A disciple is one who disciplines himself in the teachings and practices of another. The word *disciple*, much like *discipline*, comes from the Latin word *discipulus*, meaning "pupil" or "learner." It refers to someone who adopts the ways of someone else. When applied to Jesus, a disciple is someone who learns from Jesus how to live like Jesus — someone who, because of God's awakening grace, conforms his or her words and

---

1. 2 Corinthians 5:17
2. Galatians 4:5
3. 1 Corinthians 6:11
4. John 10:28
5. Ephesians 2:19
6. John 1:12
7. Colossians 2:13
8. John 3:18

ways to the words and ways of Jesus. A disciple of Jesus wants to learn from Him, through the study of God's Word, the Bible, and as we listen to others teach from it. We make the Bible part of your life every day. As the Psalmist said, "With my lips I declare all the rules of your mouth."[9]

What then is the real difference between a Christian and a disciple? A Christian is someone who has trusted Christ for forgiveness of sin and been assured of life forever with Jesus. A disciple is someone who not only meets the above definition of a Christian but is following Jesus in an effort to learn how to become more like him. In the early church, those that accepted Christ were just called disciples. As the apostle Paul was starting His ministry for example, he was seeking to make disciples. In the book of Acts, after a disturbance and attempted stoning in Iconium, we see Paul and Barnabas' focus in ministry in Derbe was not to make converts, but disciples: 'When they had preached the gospel to that city and had made many disciples.'[10] The goal of evangelism has always been to make disciples (not merely Christians), not only in the early church, but also today as we see Jesus command to us to "Go therefore and make disciples of all nations...."[11]

Characteristics of a Disciple of Jesus

As Jesus was calling His first disciples, He spoke the simple command, "Follow me."[12] A disciple is a follower, one who believes and trusts in a teacher and follows that teacher's words and example. To be a disciple is to be in a relationship. It is having an instructive, intimate, and imitative relationship with the teacher. Consequently, being a disciple of Jesus Christ is being in relationship with Jesus and seeking to be like Him. In other words, we follow Christ to be like Christ[13] because as His disciples, we belong to Christ. The disciple of Jesus has certain characteristics which differ from a 'Sunday-only' Christian in that they are commensurate with a relationship with Jesus. There are some who try to distinguish between being a Christian and being a disciple, but the Bible never makes this type of distinction. The early Christians were first called disciples. Being *Christ's disciple* and being a *Christian* are synonymous. Trusting, obeying and listening to Christ is what a Christian does. As a consequence, being a Christian is being a disciple, from the beginning until today.

---

9. Psalm 119:13
10. Acts 14:21
11. Matthew 28:19
12. Mark 1:17; 2:14; John 1:43

13. 1 Corinthians 11:1

A Disciple Listens to Jesus

One could never claim to be a disciple of a teacher without being ready to listen to that teacher. The world is full of teachers who are looking for followers and listeners! A disciple of Jesus listens to Him and when Jesus speaks, the disciple listens. The disciple clings to every word of the Master as if that word were bread for the hungry or water for the thirsty. When Jesus gathered together His disciples on the Mount of Transfiguration, God the Father spoke from heaven with a clear command: "This is my beloved Son, with whom I am well pleased; listen to him."[14] To be a Christian implies that you listen intently to Jesus.

A Disciple Learns from Jesus

We must not only listen to Jesus. A disciple does not listen and then turn away as though the teacher's words had no impact. When Jesus calls His disciples, He instructs them to learn from Him as well as to listen. When they respond to His call, He says, "Take my yoke upon you, and learn from me, for I am gentle and lowly in heart, and you will find rest for your souls."[15] To be a disciple is to be a learner, and the words of Christ carry weight. In John 6, Jesus was teaching many were grumbling at his words, which eventually led to many turning away from Jesus. He then turned to the twelve and asked "Do you want to go away as well?"[16]

Peter, speaking for the others, replied: "Lord, to whom shall we go? You have the words of eternal life, and we have believed, and have come to know, that you are the Holy One of God."[17] The disciple's greatest desire is learning from Christ and is foundational to all that he or she believes. Joyfully receiving the words of the Master as vital as daily bread, the disciple meditates upon them day and night.[18]

A Disciple Obeys Jesus

No one may call himself a disciple of Jesus who is not willing to obey Him. The disciple will put into practice what he learns from time with Jesus. Because Jesus has proven Himself worthy, not obeying Him is not an option. As I mentioned in the Introduction, Jesus himself tells us that we show Him what we think of Him and whether we love Him by our level of obedience. A passage in Luke 6 always resonates very powerfully to me. Jesus uses an analogy of building a house on either a weak or strong foundation, and then He states, "Why do you call me 'Lord, Lord,'

---

14. Matthew 17:5
15. Matthew 11:29
16. Matthew 6:67
17. John 6:68-69

18. Psalm 1:2

and not do what I tell you? Everyone who comes to me and hears my words and does them, I will show you what he is like: he is like a man building a house, who dug deep and laid the foundation on the rock."[19]

Examining Yourself

As we come to Christ, we are explicitly called to be disciples of Jesus and not just lukewarm Christians. The question then quickly may come to mind, 'But what exactly does a disciple look like? And how am I supposed to know if I am a disciple of Jesus?' I am attempting to answer these questions through this book and will focus on them specifically in Chapter 8. Traditionally, a disciple of biblical times would learn from a teacher, and in the case of the Christian life, an older man who had been discipled himself would commit himself to discipling a few younger men and training them up in the ways of a disciple of Jesus. I have committed much of my life to this process, based on Paul's admonition in 2 Timothy chapter 2. As I was discipled by Brad Miller, the Navigator staff member who initially invested in my life, I then wanted to invest my life in the lives of younger men myself. "What you have heard from me in the presence of many witnesses entrust to faithful men," Paul wrote to young Timothy, "who will be able to teach others also."[20] Through this verse and others, I've developed this definition of discipleship:

Discipling others is the process by which a Christian **with a life worth reproducing** commits himself for an extended period of time to a few individuals who have trusted Christ, the purpose being to aid and guide their growth to maturity and equip them to **reproduce themselves in a third spiritual generation**.

Because this process is not often valued in the western church, I offer these Six Marks of a Disciple of Jesus. The Six Marks of a Disciple detailed in this book are given as a way to 'examine yourself,' to see how you are doing in each of these six areas, take corrective action where necessary, and find a band of other disciples to hold you accountable in the areas where you need it. In 2 Corinthians, Paul gives us a great admonition in this area, 'examine yourselves, to see whether you are in the faith. Test yourselves. Or do you not realize this about yourselves, that Jesus Christ is in you?—unless indeed you fail to meet the test!'[21] May the chapters that follow be a good 'examination' of whether you are in the faith! My heart's desire is that as you find victory in these Six Marks in your own life, you too would take what you've learned and apply the 2 Timothy 2 principle, investing into the lives

---

19. Luke 6:46-48
20. 2 Timothy 2:2
21. 2 Corinthians 13:5

of many others whom God brings into your life.

Why we should be Disciples of Jesus

Over the last few years, I have enjoyed a series of YouTube videos from a company called EnChroma that makes special glasses that allow individuals who are color blind to see color for the first time. If you haven't seen the videos, go to the EnChroma website and watch a few. You will see people who has been colorblind for their whole lives put on the glasses for the first time and see colors in the same way the rest of us do every day. There are several connecting characteristics of each of these videos: Most of the time, these glasses are given as a gift—a surprise to the recipients—and their families arrange for them to be outdoors or in a colorful setting when they see bright, beautiful colors for the first time in their lives. When the colorblind loved one puts on the glasses and sees colors they've never seen before, they begin to cry. The flood of a rainbow of colors they've never seen before is too much for their emotions to contain, after a lifetime of seeing the world in shades of gray. Age and gender don't seem to matter: men and women, old and young all begin to cry once they see color for the very first time!

When we surrender our lives to Christ, we should also feel so overwhelmed with joy at what God has done for us through Christ! These Six Marks should not be burdens for us to carry, for we know through Christ, His burdens are light. It was the apostle John who wrote in 1 John "For this is the love of God, that we keep his commandments. And his commandments are not burdensome." Becoming more like Jesus is both for our good and His glory! That is how He intended our lives to be lived!

Jonathan Edwards explains the concept this way: "And in communicating his fullness for them, he does it for himself, because their good, which he seeks, is so much in union and communion with himself. God is their good. Their excellency and happiness are nothing but the emanation and expression of God's glory."[22]

In other words, our best life is lived as we seek deep communion with God, and His glory is revealed as we grow more like Jesus. For many of us, when we reflect deeply upon how we were rescued and redeemed from eternity separated from God forever, we find ourselves in a very emotional experience!

The challenge of obedience to God's commands for many of us is that we do not have a good filter by which to trust that God is good and that He loves us. In

---

22. Edwards, Jonathan; The End for Which God Created the World. Kyros Press.

the pages that follow, you will read a number of commands that God has given us to obey and for some, these commands might feel like legalism reborn, like a retreat from the grace found in the finished work of the cross. And yes, while I believe that our salvation is won by faith alone and through Christ alone, the apostle Paul also tells us in Philippians to 'work out your own salvation with fear and trembling, for it is God who works in you, both to will and to work for his good pleasure.'[23] And so we work it out, fully knowing that Jesus loves us completely and trusting in what Jesus commands us to do. These commands are not an example of God lording His authority over us; rather, because we can see the intensity of God's love for us, we trust that He wants the best for us. As Todd Wagner writes in his book *Come and See*, 'Somehow, we fall into the trap of thinking that following God's commands will lead to no good thing instead of reminding ourselves continually that[24] 'no good thing does He withhold from those who walk uprightly.'[25]

As you read these Six Marks and learn from God's word in each chapter, remember that God wants you to be more like Jesus and has provided this plan for us all. Take the instruction found within this book as a guide toward Christlikeness.

First Steps to Becoming a Disciple of Jesus

Jesus wants you to be His disciple because doing so leads to an abundant life! Abandonment of your own will to His commands leads to this abundant life, full of purpose and joy. I hope you use this book to draw yourself into a new level in your relationship with Jesus, and also that you are able to share this journey with a community of like-minded believers who want to walk this path together with you.

As you prepare to begin this journey, examine your current life with Christ and see if you consider yourself to currently be just a convert or a true disciple of Jesus. If your self-analysis draws you to conclude that you are only a convert, why? What has been keeping you from really following and obeying Jesus? Get a sheet of paper or pick up your journal and write down your thoughts and some of the areas you'd like to improve in as you go through this study with others.

---

23. Philippians 2:12-13
24. Wagner, Todd; Come and See. 1st Edition; David C. Cook, 2017
25. Psalm 84:11

Self-Reflection Questions

1. What is the most significant part of your own testimony of how you came to Christ?

2. As you recall your conversion to following Christ, what factors led to you to go from convert to disciple of Jesus

3. Do you believe you are able to listen to Jesus? If so, what does that look like?

4. If you were to take a step forward in discipleship, what might that look like and what difference might that make for you?

Group Discussion Questions

5. How does the explanation in this chapter of the difference between a Christian and a disciple of Jesus strike you?

6. As you read the characteristics of a disciple of Jesus in this chapter, what can you most relate to in your own life?

7. Have you had anyone disciple you and/or have you discipled others, helping them grow in their daily walk with Jesus? If so, describe that process for others in your grou

8. Talk about the connection Jesus makes in John 14:15 between our love for Him and how well we obey Him, where He said, 'If you love me, you will follow my commands.' How does that motivate you, and in what direction?

Chapter 2

The First Mark of a Disciple of Jesus

Identified with Christ

I love helping out with the regular errands that need to be done for our family, as one way that I can be a blessing to those I love. Doing the grocery shopping is one of the main ways I can help out at home. My wife and I love "Sam's Club," an American chain of member-only retail warehouse stores, as we value the opportunity it affords to buy in bulk which is especially helpful for our family of five. One recent trip to Sam's Club stands out in my mind. As I stood waiting in the checkout line to pay for my items, I could hear a man behind me in line who was speaking Chinese.

(If you and I have not already met, there are two things in the context of this story that you need to know about me. First, I am conversationally fluent in Chinese, thanks to my Asian Studies Bachelor's degree, the year we lived in China for an intensive language study program and the many hours spent studying Chinese and speaking Chinese with Chinese friends on my many trips to China for ministry. Secondly, I'm quite tall: 6 feet 7 inches!)

As this Chinese man talked on his phone, I could understand his entire conversation! (It helped that he was speaking loudly, making it easier for me to hear him.) He probably did not think any of the Americans within earshot could understand his conversation with his friend, as he complained in Chinese, "Yeah,

I'm just standing in line at Sam's Club and it's taking forever! I don't know what's taking so long. And on top of that, there's this huge mountain of a man in front of me!" That man was me!

Although I don't always reveal to Chinese living in America that I know and can understand Chinese, the opportunity here was too rich! So, as he disconnected the call, I waited a moment, then turned around and said to him in Chinese, 'Hi friend! Where are you from in China?'

At that moment, I could tell that a few things were happening in his brain simultaneously. First, he was likely thinking, "Man, this guy's Chinese is good," simultaneously with "That means he probably could understand what I was saying on the phone!?!" Likely, those thoughts were quickly followed by, "…and I just insulted him during my phone conversation with my friend!"

As you may know, one rarely sees people of Asian heritage blush; it's just not in their skin tone. But just as sure as I'm writing these words to you now, this Chinese man was blushing like I've never seen before! He meekly said to me in Chinese, "Hello friend, your Chinese is quite good. Where did you study?' We proceeded to have a nice conversation in Chinese about his hometown and my living and working experience in China until it was time for me to check out and pay for my bulk goods.

I love telling that story, and it's particularly appropriate for the topic at hand. Although I ended up revealing my identity to him—that I can understand and speak Chinese and that I have a good understanding of Chinese history and culture—it would have been just as easy to not say anything to him, continuing to wait in line until it was time to check out and hide my full identity as an Anglo-American who can speak Chinese.

I'm afraid that in our modern Western Church, far too many of us are also hiding our identities. We may attend church on Sunday, maybe we go to an event or two during the week at our church, but we do not—every day—fully identify as a disciple of Jesus, as one who has accepted Him as Lord of our everyday lives.

The first mark of a disciple of Jesus is that they have identified with the person of Jesus Christ—willing to openly admit that they belong to Christ. At one point in His ministry, Jesus asked the disciples, "Who do you say that I am?" Peter answered,

"You are the Christ."[1] A disciple seizes on the opportunity to identify himself with Jesus Christ.

So as we look at being identified with Christ, we must examine three parts of this key identifying mark: (1) we must know Jesus intimately and have an abiding relationship with Him before we can identify with Him; (2) we must wrestle (in a healthy way) with who are in Christ as a key to identifying with Him; and finally, (3) we must look at what it means to fully identify with Christ.

Knowing Jesus Intimately

Beyond a doubt, the apostle Paul is one of my favorite biblical characters and one of my heroes of the faith. His unyielding patience and persistence to preach Christ, and his exhortation to others to live for Jesus are examples for us all. The late 19th Century German theologian Adolf Deissmann declared about Paul, "'There is no single person since Nero's days who has left such permanent marks on the souls of men as Paul the New Man." [2] I believe one of those 'permanent marks' was Paul's sold-out determination to live for and love Jesus. In Philippians 3, Paul states, 'But whatever gain I had, I counted as loss for the sake of Christ. Indeed, I count everything as loss because of the surpassing worth of knowing Christ Jesus my Lord. For his sake I have suffered the loss of all things and count them as rubbish, in order that I may gain Christ and be found in him, not having a righteousness of my own that comes from the law, but that which comes through faith in Christ, the righteousness from God that depends on faith—that I may know him.'[3] I have invested countless hours memorizing and meditating on this verse, and each time I revisit it, I am blown away by what it would really mean for me to 'count as loss' everything I have, own or treasure for the sake of Christ! Jesus makes the point even clearer when He says in Luke 14:33, 'So therefore, any one of you who does not renounce all that he has cannot be my disciple.'

Renouncing all we have (counting all as loss) seems like it should be basic Christianity—but in practical terms, it is so hard to do! During our conversion, we receive and believe in Jesus, forsaking all other things, placing Him in the #1 position of our lives. Jesus tells us about this in a parable found in Matthew 13. 'The kingdom of heaven is like treasure hidden in a field, which a man found and covered up. Then in his joy he goes and sells all that he has and buys that field.' This is a "parable-way" of explaining the same truth: selling and giving everything

---

1. Mark 8:29
2. Jackson, Wayne. Some Character Traits of Paul, the Apostle, https://www.christiancourier.com/articles/1385-some-character-traits-of-paul-the-apostle
3. Philippians 3:7-10

you have with joy and counting everything as loss in order to gain Christ. But in practical terms, how is this experienced in our lives? I think there are at least four ways in our lives that provide good starting points for what it means to *renounce all and count it as loss:*

1. If a choice is needed between Christ and anything else, we will choose Christ.
2. As decisions, priorities or situations arise in our lives, we will deal with them in ways that draw us nearer to Christ, so that we gain more of and enjoy more of Christ.
3. We will deal with the things of this world in ways that show they are not our treasure, but rather, Christ is our treasure.
4. When we suffer loss of things, whether material or otherwise, we will not lose our joy! Christ alone will be our joy and our treasure in life.

Our Identity in Christ

As we try to identify why so many of us struggle with fully committing our lives to Christ, the answer is quite simple: it comes down to identity, that search all humans have to find out who we are. What does it mean to be "who you are?" Identity relates to our basic values that dictate the choices we make. These choices then reflect who we are and what we value. For example, we can assume that a high school teacher values education and helping students, while an investment banker values money.

And for the believers in Jesus who desire to find their true identity in Christ alone, this topic of identity becomes even more pointed. If we find our identity in our career or our accomplishments, we will always need to acomplish more to find self-worth. If we listen to what others say about us and allow their opinions to determine our identity, we will always be seeking to please other people instead of God our Father. How we identify ourselves determines how we approach life.

As we seek our identity, we also have an enemy who emphatically desires to distort what we think of ourselves. He wants desperately to erase our understanding of who we really are in Christ as a part of the spiritual war on our identity.

This spiritual attack on our identity calls for a focus of our attention at this point. As I have examined the nature of our enemy Satan, we know that he cannot create anything. Only God can do that! So instead, Satan can only try to pervert, distort and destroy what God has already created. In John 10, we read that 'The thief comes only to steal and kill and destroy.'[4] And in this battle, his first target is God's children—us! As all good parents agree, if you want to try to hurt me and get to me, going after one of my three children would be the place to start. I love my kids so much and don't want anything bad to ever happen to them. In much the same way, as Satan goes after us and after our identity, his strategy is to attack us as God's beloved children.

The enemy's clear strategy here is that if he can distort who we really are and disrupt our identity in Christ, he has won! That's what he wanted to accomplish! How does he typically do this? Many times, he works through the opinions of others, through hurt and pain. and through the unrealistic expectations that media and culture place on us.

In this battle for our minds, Satan tries to put thoughts in our heads. We all know this battle as we have heard these attacks:

- 'I'm not good enough to earn God's acceptance and love'
- 'I'm not important to anyone'
- 'I'll never amount to anything….'

And then he attacks even deeper:

- 'You know that sin you committed, you could never be forgiven *for that one.*'
- 'What about that failed marriage or failed business, how could God continue to love you after that?'
- 'You never do anything right….'

Sound familiar?

And here's the kicker: You know he has won the battle when he gets *you* to repeat the accusations that he planted in your mind.

If these lies of Satan hit a little too close to home, I have really good news for you! We do not have to permanently live in these lies. God thinks of you much differently than Satan would have you believe! Through Christ, our identity looks

---

4. John 10:10

much different. Look through and study this incomplete list of who the Bible says we are through Christ.

In Christ, we are
- A new creation in Christ (2 Corinthians 5:17)
- His workmanship, created in Christ Jesus for good works (Ephesians 2:10)
- No longer condemned (Romans 8:1)
- Children of God (Galatians 3:26)
- Holy temples (1 Corinthians 6:19)
- Overcomers (Romans 8:37)
- Loved by God (1 Thessalonians 1:4)
- Not given a spirit of fear, but of power, love and self-control
- Friends of Jesus (John 15:14)
- Children of light, children of the day. We are not of the night or of the darkness (1 Corinthians 5:5)
- Ambassadors of Christ (2 Corinthians 5:20)
- God's masterpieces (Ephesians 2:10)
- Seated with him in the heavenly places in Christ Jesus (Ephesians 2:6)
- Able to do all things through him who strengthens us. (Philippians 4:13)

- Recipients of the peace of God, which surpasses all understanding, and will guard our hearts and our minds in Christ Jesus (Philippians 4:7)
- God's chosen ones, holy and beloved (Ephesians 1:4)
- Wise and restored (I Corinthians 1:30)

Take a moment to just pause and reflect. Look through the list again. If you repeated this list to yourself each morning when you awake, replacing the 'We' for 'I'.... *I am God's chosen one, I am God's masterpiece, I am a new creation in Christ*, etc., how would that change how you identify or think of yourself? I believe that every day we get to choose if we identify with Satan's version of us, or with what the Bible says we are through Christ.

And if we really are who the Bible says we are, how should that affect how we identify ourselves to the world?

Being Identified with Christ

My life, perhaps like yours, has been full of ups and downs as I've made my way to where I find myself today. One of the most important times of my life happened while I was in my early 20's. I grew up in a fairly dysfunctional home with a Mom who, as I found out much later, suffered severe depression through most of my childhood, and a Dad was a workaholic and never knew how to connect to me or my brother. Because of all the dysfunction at home, I found solace within the youth ministry that friends invited me to join, and during my senior year of high school, I trusted Christ as my Savior. When I left home for college, I had only made it 2 ½ years into my time at Colorado State University when my parents divorced, a decision that dried up my support system at home as well as the funding my Dad had committed for my education.

Because I hadn't graduated from university, I had few skills suitable for the workplace and found my first job first selling cars, then doing telephone marketing calls for a small local company. During this season I began to discover that my spiritual gifting enabled me to start new ventures easily, and I began to see God at work through my efforts. I soon started a single adult ministry in Fort Collins, Colorado called Cornerstone Bible Fellowship. I enjoyed the challenge of figuring out the nuances of starting the ministry and began to find opportunities to speak at local churches about our new venture and to invite the single adults in these congregations to join our Bible studies and Wednesday night 'service' for single adults. After one such speaking event at a Baptist church, a mustached 'older' man came up to me and asked me if I would like to grab coffee sometime after work to talk more about our ministry. I heartily agreed to the meeting with Brad Miller, given that although I enjoyed the start-up nature of what I was doing, I also realized that I could certainly use some help in relation to the Bible study and other theological parts of our ministry, having come to Christ myself just a few years before.

As we found time in our schedule for the meeting, I learned quickly that Brad enjoyed hearing about our new ministry and wanted to learn more. He too had a heart for single adult ministry and in his capacity with The Navigators, he was investing both in the lives of college students at Colorado State University and in young men in Fort Collins. He wanted to know if I was interested in meeting weekly, the beginning of a discipleship relationship. At the time that I agreed to start meeting with Brad, I had no idea how impactful those times together would be! The several years that he and I met together not only changed my young relationship with Jesus but would shape the course of the rest of my life.

I had never known an adult man to be so concerned about my mental and spiritual well-being. His tender and sometimes tough love for me set me on a course that would lead to joining the Navigators myself, meeting my wife (a single Navigator staff member herself) and into a life of impacting Asians for Christ. I often tell Brad that the 350,000+ Chinese we've seen come to know Christ through our ministry are largely because of what God did through him in my life.[5] I cannot imagine what my life would now be like without Brad's involvement and intervention at a time that I was struggling to understand God's will for my life.

Many of you have similar stories of people who invested in your life at time when their influence was needed most. As you can imagine, I would do anything for his man after what he has done for me! If he needed someone to help him move, I would be the first to drive the 90 minutes to his house to help. If Brad were to need help or assistance in any way, I would be there to help him in a heartbeat! And if he goes home to heaven before me, I will change whatever plans I have for that week to be there to honor this man's life and the impact he has had on me.

Are you able to relate to the way I feel about Brad? Think for a minute about someone who may have had this kind of impact on your life. Who comes to mind? Your appreciation for them is a powerful feeling, isn't it?

Now, think about how much more God has done for you through your relationship with Jesus Christ! Jesus took your place on the Cross and took on the wrath of God for your sin. He laid down his life for us, reconciled us to God, and as we read in Colossians 2, 'And you, who were dead in your trespasses and the uncircumcision of your flesh, God made alive together with him, having forgiven us all our trespasses, by canceling the record of debt that stood against us with its legal demands. This He set aside, nailing it to the cross. He disarmed the rulers and authorities and put them to open shame, by triumphing over them in him.'[6]

After all that Jesus has done for us, how much more should we give everything we have and everything we are to Him? The apostle Paul—the best example I know of someone who fully identified with Christ--says it best in Galatians 2 when he writes, 'I have been crucified with Christ. It is no longer I who live, but Christ who lives in me. And the life I now live in the flesh I live by faith in the Son of

---

5. An interesting side note: my oldest daughter got involved with the Navigators her freshman year in college, and this same man who had invested in my life is now overseeing all Navigators ministry in the Rocky Mountain region, including the ministry where my daughter is an active participant! How wonderful that she is now participating in a ministry he oversees!
6. Colossians 2:13-15

God, who loved me and gave himself for me.' It is this type of surrender to Christ and identification of who are in Christ that God wants for us, too!

Just as I could have camouflaged myself to the Chinese man at Sam's Club, we can choose to camouflage ourselves to the world, or we can identify ourselves with our Savior so there will be no doubt in anyone's mind that we have devoted our lives to following Christ. By taking Paul's admonition in Romans 1 that '…I am not ashamed of the gospel, for it is the power of God for salvation to everyone who believes, to the Jew first and also to the Greek.'[7]

Can you say this is true in your life as well?

First Steps Toward Fully Identifying with Jesus

As I mentioned at the beginning of this chapter, we must know who Jesus is and have an intimacy with Him before we can identify with Him. This kind of relationship begins by investing in regular time with Him. You can recognize the voices of your loved ones even in a pitch-dark room because you've spent a lot of time with them and you know the familiarity of each voice. It's the same way with Jesus!

Getting into the habit of daily time with Him will be helpful for getting to know Him, to know His voice and the ways that He is working in and through you. I have developed the habit of an additional "Time Alone With God on Fridays (I call it a "T.A.W.G.!"). In this time frame of two to three hours each Friday, I prepare myself to learn to hear His voice through a combination of Scripture reading, praying and sometimes singing.

You might also consider using the list of 'Who we really are in Christ' (earlier in this chapter) and writing a few of those down on a paper that you can keep by your bed or taped on a mirror where you'll see it often. Study and memorize the verses, then repeat the points to yourself as you are getting ready for the day. Allow the Lord to let the point sink in until you know it's true and believe it in your heart!

---

7. Romans 1:16

Discussion Questions

Self-Reflection Questions

1. Where are you right now in your walk with Jesus? Full-on devotee? Interested but not yet devoted?

2. How are you doing in your pursuit to know Jesus intimately?

3. In what ways do you struggle with answering the question, 'Who am I?'

4. As you consider your identity in Christ and what He has done for you, what are you thankful for?

Group Discussion Questions

5. As you re-read through the list of who you really are in Christ, which points need further examination in relation to your fully accepting yourself in that way?

6. According to the points you made for the previous question, how should that affect how we identify ourselves to the world?

7. What are the biggest obstacles for you to fully identify with Jesus in every area of your life?

8. What help do you need from this group as you seek to identify fully as a disciple of Jesus?

Chapter 3

The Second Mark of a Disciple of Jesus

Supreme Love for Jesus

I have many different kinds of "loves" in my life. I tend to be someone who runs either really hot or really cold toward specific things, and out of all the people or things that I love (my wife and kids, lasagna, the movie Fletch, anything that has chocolate, bananas, my dog, coffee, etc.), I love the Bible more than any of those things. I love to read it in the morning, read it at night, memorize it, talk to people about it, teach from it, see God use our ministry to translate it into other languages, study it for hours at a time and tell others about it. I want to be someone who knows God's Word intimately and who obeys it completely. In my own study of the Bible, I've written my own white papers (statements on theological topics) and shared them with others when requested. As you'll read in Chapter 4 of this book, I believe beyond any doubt that the Bible is the inspired Word of God and that it is worth our time to know it well.

As I've thoroughly studied the Bible, I believe there is really no clearer theological principle in the Bible than God's desire for us to have a supreme, undying, incorruptible and incomparable love for Jesus, which is the second Mark of a Disciple of Jesus. This important theological principle is also very complex, so let's dive right into the topic by looking at Matthew 22, where we'll see Jesus teaching the crowds as both the Pharisees and Sadducees questioned Jesus.

Throughout the Gospels, two main groups of people were in almost constant conflict with Jesus and His disciples. These two groups, the Sadducees and Pharisees, comprised the ruling class of Jews in Israel at the time of Jesus.

Both groups were religious sects within Judaism and had some similarities, including both honoring Moses and the Law and both having a measure of political power, but there were differences as well. The Sadducees were more conservative in their interpretation of the text of Scripture (which at the time was only what we know as the Old Testament), whereas the Pharisees gave oral tradition equal authority to the written Word of God.

This conservative interpretation of Scripture is what the Sadducees were trying to use to trip up Jesus in Matthew 22 with a question on the Resurrection, which they did not believe in. When Jesus was able to silence them, the Pharisees stepped up with a question of their own. In Matthew 22:36, we read, "Teacher, which is the great commandment in the Law?" And He [Jesus] said to him, "You shall love the Lord your God with all your heart and with all your soul and with all your mind. This is the great and first commandment. And a second is like it: You shall love your neighbor as yourself. On these two commandments depend all the Law and the Prophets."[1]

Notice that, in verse 35, the Pharisees chose a 'lawyer' to ask the question about which commandment was greatest, which in that day would have been an expert in Old Testament Law. The Pharisees truly hated Jesus and wanted to do anything they could do trip Him up and discredit his ministry. They hated Jesus not because He called them names, but because He threatened everything they stood for, everything they were working toward, including their prestige and their income. In order to try to prove He was a fraud, they tried tripping up Jesus with a test.

Why is this question about "which commandment is greatest" a test? The Old Testament Law actually listed 613 Commandments! The smartest experts of the Law often argued over this, and they strongly disagreed among themselves about the answer. By asking Jesus this question they thought they had Him cornered—right where they wanted him!

---

1. Matthew 22:36-40

Jesus's answer came directly out of the Old Testament Law itself, "You shall love the Lord your God with all your heart and with all your soul and with all your mind. This is the great and first commandment." Originally from Deuteronomy 6, Jesus made it really simple: Love God with all you have, this is the greatest commandment, the first demand of Jesus.

What does it look like in our lives to love the Lord with all we have? Jesus also makes the answer to that question pretty simple as well. In another teaching session with a group of Pharisees who were questioning Jesus, He stated, "If God were your Father, you would love me, for I came from God and I am here. I came not of my own accord, but He sent me."[2]

As we consider these two stories together, what do we see? First, the greatest command is to love God with everything we have, and as we do that, to love Jesus also with everything we have because Jesus came from God—and if we love God with everything, we love Jesus with everything!

Most amazing to me about both of these stories is what He is saying to the people who were the most religious, most God-oriented, Old Testament-saturated people on the planet at that time: *You don't know God.* He is not your Father. In fact, He even tells them that they are of their father the devil.[3] That is mind-boggling!

What is the litmus test for knowing whether somebody is a lover of God? The answer is found in how they reply to this question: Do they love Jesus? Do they embrace Jesus for who He really is? Not just as some human teacher, not just as some prophet alongside other prophets, but as the very Son of God.

Jesus calls us—as His disciples--to love Him more than we love anything else, including those within our own family (which we'll investigate deeper in Chapter 7). In Matthew 10, Jesus wants to make sure we understand His point. In a teaching session with the disciples as He is sending them out for ministry, He states,

> "Whoever loves father or mother more than me is not worthy of me, and whoever loves son or daughter more than me is not worthy of me. And whoever does not take his cross and follow me is not worthy of me. Whoever finds his life will lose it, and whoever loses his life for my sake will find it."[4]

In what may be Jesus's most 'in your face' moment, He raises His expectation of our love for Him to a very personal level.

---

2. John 8:42
3. John 8:44
4. Matthew 10:37-39

My family, like almost all of us would agree, is among the most important parts of my life. I loved my parents, I love my wife and children, and would do just about anything for any of them. For Jesus to say, 'Nope, you have to love me more' is a bold statement that we should take very seriously.

So, what does this love really look like?

Loving Jesus singularly and selflessly

To love Jesus above all others is to love Him to a degree that you're willing to deny yourself, abandon everything you have, even hate yourself. According to His Word, you must be willing to say goodbye to your family, your friends, your fortune--all for the sake of Jesus. This is what it means to love Him singularly! We must love Him so that we desire to obey Him, to honor Him, to serve Him and to proclaim Him.

A key verse that I've clung to for almost as long as I have been a disciple of Jesus is Paul's admonition in Galatians 2. This was one of the first verses that I memorized, and it has served as a guide in my walk with Jesus for over thirty years. As you read this passage, think about what would need to be true of your life for you to be able to say this about yourself: "I have been crucified with Christ. It is no longer I who live, but Christ who lives in me. And the life I now live in the flesh I live by faith in the Son of God, who loved me and gave himself for me."[5]

In order to check my own love for Christ and so that I can say that 'it is no longer I who live, but Christ who lives in me,' I have developed a checklist, originally taken from a list by John Piper,[6] that I use nearly every day as I start out toward a new day. I share it here that you may add it to your own routine and that you may use it to check where you land in your own singular love of Jesus. How many of these statements can you say are true for you today?

- I *admire* Jesus Christ more than any other human or angelic being.
- I *enjoy* his ways and his words more than I enjoy the ways and words of anyone else.
- I *want his approval* more than I want the approval of anyone else.[7]
- I *want to be with him* more than I want to be with anyone else.
- I *feel more grateful* to him for what He has done for me than I do to anyone else.

---

5. Galatians 2:20
6. Piper, John. I love Jesus Christ. https://www.desiringgod.org/articles/i-love-jesus-christ
7. Galatians 1:10

- I *trust* his words more fully than I trust what anyone else says.
- I am *more glad in his exaltation* than in the exaltation of anyone else, including me.

When you are able to say and know that these statements are generally true for you, then you have begun to have a singularly and selfless love for Jesus.

A love for Jesus that is not subject to being corrupted

In our world today, we would consider very few things to be incorruptible. In fact, most things in our world are subject to corruption, mostly because of our fallen world and the sin-saturated people who inhabit it. We see corruption everywhere in our politics, in those running national, state and local governments, in our businesses and yes, even in our churches. Even things we own, such as electronics are subject to corruption. If people or things are corrupt, they are broken in some way. Corrupt people perform illegal or immoral acts for personal gain, without apology. When you corrupt someone, you convince them to do something wrong or illegal. If you talk your little sister into stealing candy from a cupboard, you are corrupting her. If something is corrupt, it is rotten, spoiled or out of commission, like a file that makes your computer crash.

In the last verse of the book of Ephesians, the apostle Paul, as he often does at the end of his letters, offers words of grace by writing, "Grace be with all who love our Lord Jesus Christ with love incorruptible."[8] Various English Bible translations translate the Greek word *aphtharsia* differently, but the concept is a love without end, with purity and sincerity, and yes, an incorrupt love. So how are we to have a love for Jesus that is incorruptible?

First Steps toward a Supreme Love For Christ

Three key thoughts come to mind when I think of a few First Steps on how we can have this kind of never-ending, pure and sincere love for Jesus.

1. Determine who Jesus really is

The opinions about Jesus are many in today's world. Many believe that He

---

8. Ephesians 6:24

existed, but that He is not the Son of God. Others believe that He was a good teacher and brought some good values to human history through His teaching. In modern-day China, as I assume we may see in many places around the world, a growing group of intellectuals and high society types are often called 'Cultural Christians' because they adhere to Christian values and appreciate Christian culture based on the benefits to their daily lives, but do not place their lives under the Lordship of Jesus.

C.S. Lewis described the inherent foolishness of claiming Christ as nothing more than a good teacher in his classic book *Mere Christianity*. He wrote:

> "I am trying here to prevent anyone saying the really foolish thing that people often say about Him: "I'm ready to accept Jesus as a great moral teacher, but I don't accept his claim to be God." That is the one thing we must not say. A man who was merely a man and said the sort of things Jesus said would not be a great moral teacher. He would either be a lunatic—on the level with the man who says he is a poached egg—or else he would be the Devil of Hell. You must make your choice. Either this man was, and is, the Son of God, or else a madman or something worse. You can shut him up for a fool, you can spit at him and kill him as a demon or you can fall at his feet and call him Lord and God. But let us not come with any patronizing nonsense about his being a great human teacher. He has not left that open to us. He did not intend to."[9]

You will not have a pure and enduring love for Jesus until you settle the question about who He is in your mind and in your heart. As C.S. Lewis states, there are only three options as answers to the question: Liar, Lunatic or Lord. If He was a Liar or a Lunatic, He isn't worth our time to pursue Him, but if we look at all the evidence and determine that He is the Son of God, then we must make Him also Lord of our lives. This is expressed so well by the apostle Peter, "Though you have not seen him, you love him. Though you do not now see him, you believe in him and rejoice with joy that is inexpressible and filled with glory, obtaining the outcome of your faith, the salvation of your souls."[10] As we settle the question of who He is, the outcome of our faith in Him results in a joy inexpressible as we rejoice in who He is and how much He loves us!

---

9. Lewis, C.S. Mere Christianity, Harper Collins
10. I Peter 1:8-9

2. Recall what He has done in your own life

As I have discipled men and led Bible studies, one of the tools I want to make sure every Christian has is a good understanding of the story of how they came to faith in Jesus. We often call this our 'testimony'—simply the story of how we came to believe in Jesus. I often tell people that our testimony is the "Here is who I was before I knew Jesus, here is how I came to know and accept Jesus, and the here is who I am after accepting Jesus" story of our lives. Having a solid testimony can be a very powerful tool for evangelism and witnessing because no one can argue with your own story. It's the account of real-life events that happened to you![11]

Recalling the story of what God did in and through your life as you found and accepted Jesus is very beneficial toward having a solid and incorruptible love for Jesus. It's easy for us to forget what Jesus did in those early days of discovery and acceptance of Jesus' love for us, especially for those who have been Christians for a long time. The incorruptible love that Jesus has for us is what motivates us, even compels us to give Jesus our whole heart with a love that is lasting.

Peter captures the duality of this part of our relationship with Jesus in the book of 1 Peter as he writes, 'Blessed be the God and Father of our Lord Jesus Christ! According to his great mercy, He has caused us to be born again to a living hope through the resurrection of Jesus Christ from the dead, to an inheritance that is imperishable (same Greek word here as 'incorruptible'), undefiled, and unfading, kept in heaven for you, who by God›s power are being guarded through faith for a salvation ready to be revealed in the last time. In this you rejoice…"[12] Think about what Peter is saying here for just a moment. Yes, blessings to God for what He has done for us in Christ!

Jesus saved us from an eternity separated from God and gave us an inheritance that will never end, is perfect in every way and is waiting for us in heaven until we arrive! Wow! Christian, rejoice! As we really meditate on this, our reaction should be 'Jesus, praise your name! Thank you! I love you so much!'

3. Rearrange Your Priorities Correspondingly

After you determine who Jesus is and that Jesus is Lord of your life and recall all that has been done for you through Christ and what is waiting for you in heaven, the next step is an essential one: rearranging your priorities to reflect those realities. Here is an important truth that I've learned about life: We will spend most of our

---

11. If you've never thought through your testimony, a worksheet is included in the Resources section to help you think through your story and be able to have it ready when you want to share it with others!
12. 1 Peter 1:3-6

time on the values that are most important to us. Indian Activist Mahatma Gandhi once said that our 'actions express our priorities,' and I think he was right.[13] It is from this principle that I took the title of this book.

A disciple of Jesus will show the Marks outlined in this book, if they are, in fact, a disciple of Jesus. Truly, what you do shows who you are! When I begin meeting with someone for the first time to help them toward spiritual growth, I can pretty accurately tell what that person values and where they spend their time in the first 30 minutes of our meeting together. It then gives me a starting place as I begin to help them grow in their walk with the Lord. Do they say that they love God and hearing from Him? If so, they will tell me of their spiritual discipline of time in God's Word and time in prayer. Do I hear 'I love my wife and kids' from them? If so, I will also most likely hear of the intentional time he is spending with them. And when I hear, 'I love Jesus with my whole heart,' I also expect to hear of all the evangelistic and outreach events they are a part of and the ways they've rearranged how they run their business, how they spend their time and their money.

Jesus said, 'For where your treasure is, there your heart (your time, talent and treasure) will be also.'[14]

Go back to the checklist I provided earlier in the chapter. Take some time to meditate on what areas of the list you may need to address, rearranging your priorities to make it possible for every one of those items to be true of you.

Finally, one last note about priorities: I think we all completely understand that as people, we're not perfect. Even as we've been made as 'new creations or creatures,'[15] we're still on a path toward complete renewal. We all wrestle with habitual sins and recurring rebellion every single day! So, if you're feeling a little overwhelmed right now, please know there is no limit to God's grace. As we determine who Jesus is and recall what's He done, that truth should spur us on to love Him back with everything we have—and this may be an up-and-down process. From my perspective, it's about intent, about putting your best effort forward to prioritize your life and the values you want your life to reflect that are important to you. As Jesus said in Luke 12, 'And do not seek what you are to eat and what you are to drink, nor be worried. For all the nations of the world seek after these things, and your Father knows that you need them. Instead, seek his kingdom, and these things will be added to you.[16] Seek his kingdom and ask Him to show you ways you can grow in your walk, and He will meet you in your journey. The biblical command is

---

13. "Ghandi Quotes." Sources of Insight. http://sourcesofinsight.com/gandhi-quotes/
14. Matthew 6:21
15. 2 Corinthians 5:17
16. Luke 12:29-31

to love God with everything we have, and the way we do that is by loving Jesus with everything we have!

Discussion Questions

Self-Reflection Questions

1. Given your love for family, how does the Matthew 10 passage (whoever loves son or daughter more than me is not worthy of me....) strike you? Hard to swallow? Understandable?

2. What items on Mike's checklist would you like to continue to work on in your own life?

3. Does the section in this chapter on Priorities convict you in a certain way? Explain.

4. Can you clearly share 'the reason for the hope that you have' in Christ through your testimony? If you have never worked on writing a clear story of how your faith began, will you work on that this week?

Group Discussion Questions

5. What is it about Jesus that most attracts you to Him?

6. We have studied in this chapter that we are called to love Jesus. What are some practical examples of ways that you can do that?

7. We love God by loving Jesus. Had you made that connection before? How does it affect what you think of both God and Jesus?

8. As you've determined who Jesus is, what determinations have you made? Do you still have questions about Jesus?

Chapter 4

The Third Mark of a Disciple of Jesus

Obedient to the Bible

One of my favorite games to play as a boy was the game *Simon Says*, a game that has been very popular with children for decades. You probably remember the game: One person is 'Simon,' and the other kids must copy what Simon says to do. Simon must always begin his command with the words, "*Simon says.*" The goal is for Simon to trick the other players into either doing something other than what Simon is doing, or doing an action when he didn't begin his sentence with the required words. If Simon says, 'Jump on your left foot,' but didn't start with the words "Simon says" and the player jumps anyway, the player is out! The last one standing is the winner and gets to be Simon for the next round. I remember playing this fun game with my friends for hours on end.

In my years of full-time ministry (since 1994), I have observed a disturbing trend among many people who identify as Christians: they do not seem to take God's word, the Bible, very seriously. For many, it seems more like a 'book of suggestions' than the living Word of God. The Christian who wants to talk about God's word and to share what God is teaching them through their time in the Bible is hard to find these days, it seems. And I've noticed that in many of our churches today, much like the game *Simon Says*, the game of 'The Bible Says' or 'Jesus Says' is a very different game.

In many of our Churches, we act as though we believe that if Jesus says to do something, you don't have to *do* it, you only have to *memorize* it. That has never made sense to me! Here's a good example: In the introduction of this book, I laid out a clear case that the Great Commission is a "normal" command for all who call themselves Christians. Through God's Word, we see Jesus giving us the commands Himself, as in Mark 16, for all Christians to 'go into all the world and proclaim the gospel to the whole creation.'[1] Later in the narrative, Jesus clearly states that if we love Him, we will do what He is commanding us to do.[2] And yet, despite the clear call to all Christians to preach the Gospel and to make disciples and show that we love Him as we do the things He commands, how many people in our churches are regularly sharing the Gospel and making disciples as a regular habit in their daily lives? However, many have *memorized* Matthew 28 about making disciples or Acts 1:8 on being Jesus' witnesses! Do they think if Jesus says to do something, you don't have to do it, you only have to memorize it! That line of thinking doesn't make sense to me!

If I tell my son to empty the dishwasher at our house, he knows that 'command' carries some weight since I am his dad and he is expected to be obedient to the things I ask him to do. Because of that shared understanding between us, he is not going to come back to me two hours after I've told him to empty the dishwasher and say to me 'Dad, I memorized what you told me to do,' without emptying the dishwasher! Nor will he come back to me and say, 'My friends are going to come over and we're going to do a study on what it would look like if I emptied the dishwasher.' He knows better than that! My son knows that when his father tells him to do something like emptying the dishwasher, he had better do it! And if he doesn't do it, there will be consequences.

I often wonder if we think we're going to stand before Jesus one day and say, "I remember all the commands you gave me to do and I memorized them." The Apostle James writes about this in James Chapter 1: 'But be doers of the word, and not hearers only, deceiving yourselves.'[3] I am certain that Jesus's follow-up question will be, "How were you at *doing them?*" We will need to have an answer for this question.

---

1. Mark 16:15
2. John 14:15
3. James 1:22

The Third Mark of a Disciple of Jesus is that he or she is obedient to the Bible, knows God's Word, and seeks to obey the commands that are found in God's Word. Your obedience shows your heart for Jesus. Far too many in our churches today are good hearers of the word, but those who are true disciples in Jesus put that "hearing" into "doing."

Perhaps you have heard of the equation: *Stated belief + actual practice = actual belief.* In this case, what you do shows what you believe about God's Word.

As a first step toward obedience to God's Word, a disciple of Jesus must have confidence in God's Word as an authoritative text that God has inspired and ordained. If the disciple wants to know God and hear from God, that communication happens primarily through the Bible. This disciple knows that God saves by the Bible, He sanctifies by the Bible, and He comforts, edifies and does all spiritual work by the Bible. The foundation of all Christian endeavor is the Word of God.

So how do aspiring disciples of Jesus come to have this confidence in God's Word? We must settle the question of whether the Bible is truly the inspired Word of God. This is key in the context of this chapter, because if it is not the inspired and authoritative Word of God, then there's no real reason to obey a false book! And while this chapter will not be an exhaustive look at the topic, consider this to be a primer. What do we mean when we say that the Bible is the inspired Word of God?

As I have studied to discern for myself whether the Bible is the inspired Word of God, the research has taken me primarily in two directions that may be helpful for you as well. First, we need to look at what the Bible says about itself; secondly, we should seek out other characteristics that we see about the Bible that may lend to answering this reliability question. The Bible says quite a bit about itself, and I'd like to focus on three passages of Scripture that are particularly helpful to understanding what the Bible says about itself.

One of my favorite Old Testament figures is Joshua, the assistant to Moses and one of the twelve spies who were called to survey the land of Canaan. Joshua's persistent obedience to Moses's requests of him is admirable, and it is no surprise that just before Moses dies, he names Joshua as the new leader of the Israelites. In Deuteronomy 34, Joshua is described as 'full of the spirit and wisdom,'[4] and in Joshua Chapter 1, as the new leader, God prepares him with a pep talk! God tells Joshua to be 'strong and courageous' on three occasions in the first chapter and

---

4. Deuteronomy 34:9

instructs him about the Old Testament law: 'This Book of the Law shall not depart from your mouth, but you shall meditate on it day and night, so that you may be careful to do according to all that is written in it. For then you will make your way prosperous, and then you will have good success.'[5]

There are a couple of notes about this passage of Scripture that should be instructive for us. As God encourages Joshua to take the Old Testament law seriously, He demonstrates His requirement for revelation through Scripture. Joshua is encouraged to not let it 'depart from his mouth,' to 'meditate on it day and night' and to 'be careful to do all that is written in it.' All three of these admonitions indicate a requirement toward total obedience! If Joshua were to adhere to all three of these admonitions, think about the actions that doing so required of him! Secondly, consider the promise of what this type of obedience produces: 'Then you will make your way prosperous and have good success.' We find this pattern throughout Scripture, that as God gives a command, He names either a consequence for disobedience and/or a reward for obedience.

Throughout the book of Acts, we read of the apostle Paul's missionary journeys to spread the gospel, and one of the places that Paul and his companion Barnabas visited was the town of Lystra. Located in modern-day Turkey, Lystra was not a particularly important town during the time of Paul. In Acts 14, we learn that some significant ministry took place there, including Paul healing a crippled man. Paul and Barnabas also preached the gospel there and a church began to grow. One family in this young church stood out as dedicated disciples of Jesus, and Paul discovered Timothy, a young believer in that family. During Paul's second visit to Lystra, this time with Silas, Paul began to recruit Timothy, who quickly became one of Paul's most trusted partners in ministry. Over time, Timothy became Paul's spiritual son, a young but gifted disciple whom Paul selected to oversee the church at Ephesus. Toward the end of Paul's life, he wrote three pastoral letters to those who were continuing the work that he started, and 2 Timothy is one of those letters that Paul wrote while in prison. As he awaited execution, he encouraged Timothy toward boldness, endurance and faithfulness in the face of false teaching. In Chapter 2, he also encouraged Timothy about God's Word:

'All Scripture is breathed out by God and profitable for teaching, for reproof, for correction, and for training in righteousness, that the man of God may be

---

[5]. Joshua 1:8

complete, equipped for every good work.⁶'

In these verses we find the most direct indication we have in Scripture about the Bible stating that it is God's Word. The phrase, 'all Scripture is God-breathed,' is generally understood to mean that God's Word has been inspired by God, that the Scripture is God's own words. Paul is talking about all of the Old Testament in these verses, and we have very good reasons for treating the New Testament as having the same God-breathed authority. Here are just a few of those reasons:

1. As Jesus was fulfilling his teaching ministry, he viewed his own teaching on par with Scripture[7] and having the authority of God. For example, in John 14, Jesus states, "Do you not believe that I am in the Father and the Father is in me? The words that I say to you I do not speak on my own authority, but the Father who dwells in me does his works."[8]
2. The apostles claimed to be inspired in their own ministry by God. In 1 Corinthians 2, Paul writes, 'And we impart this in words not taught by human wisdom but taught by the Spirit.'[9]
3. Finally, as Peter was writing in 2 Peter about Paul's letters to the churches, he refers to them as part of the authoritative Scriptures. He writes that some twist his letters "as they do the *other* Scriptures."[10]

As Paul wrote to Timothy about Scriptures having been breathed out by God, his words imply that he is referring to both the Old and New Testaments.

The book of Hebrews is one of my favorite books in the New Testament. Written by an unknown author to encourage Christians in a time of trial, the book focuses on the absolute supremacy and sufficiency of Jesus Christ. In Chapter 3, the author writes of how Jesus is supreme to Moses and gives the reader an encouragement to enter into the "rest" that is available through Christ. The author references the Israelites being led out of Egypt by Moses, and referencing a passage from Psalm 95, he reminds the readers of their unbelieving and evil hearts. Encouraging them to move toward God and away from the disobedience found in previous generations, the author writes,

> 'For the word of God is living and active, sharper than any two-edged sword, piercing to the division of soul and of spirit, of joints and of marrow, and discerning the thoughts and intentions of the heart.'[11]

---

6. 2 Timothy 3:16-17
7. Matthew 5:17-18
8. John 14:10
9. 1 Corinthians 2:13
10. 2 Peter 3:16
11. Hebrews 4:12

If you are a believer in Jesus and have invested time in God's word, you probably know how 'living and active' it can be! On many occasions, I have experienced reading a passage of Scripture at one time, then returning to it a few months later, only to have God speak to my heart in a different way when I read the passage again! Primarily because of this verse, I have noticed that I never see someone doing well in their relationship with the Lord who isn't investing regular time in God's Word. The Lord uses that time to refine and shape the believer into the man or woman of God that He wants them to be. God's Word truly does pierce soul and spirit, and discerns the thoughts and intentions of the heart, remolding us into a closer image of Jesus.

Can we now answer what God's Word says about itself? If we only begin with our summary from these three passages, we can see that the Bible says of itself that it is inspired by God, that it requires our utmost attention and that it is living and active, because it is God's Word and has the power of God's inspired Word. Because of these attributes, American President Abraham Lincoln is quoted as saying about the Bible, "I believe the Bible is the best gift God has ever given to man. All the good from The Savior of the world is communicated to us through this Book."

In my own efforts to determine if the Bible is reliable as God's Word, the second method has been research about the attributes of the Bible. I have found four attributes that are relevant to answer this question.

1. The Bible is affirmed through historical accuracy.

A career choice that I find fascinating is Biblical Archeology! Here are two examples of why it is so engaging.

When we hear the name 'Jericho,' we often think of Israelites marching, trumpets sounding and walls falling—a fantastic story of faith and victory! Until recently, archeological evidence did not seem to favor the biblical story. The Jericho of biblical times actually had two walls, as Jericho was located on a hill with the city wall built up against the city and another wall built toward the bottom of the hill. This lower wall had a retaining wall underneath it, for support. After the final trip around the city on the seventh day, according to the original Hebrew scriptures, the walls of Jericho 'fell beneath itself.' In 1950, British archaeologist Kathleen Kenyon found "fallen red bricks piling nearly to the top of the revetment (retaining wall.) These probably came from the wall on the summit of the bank and.... the brickwork above the revetment.'[12] In other words, she found large mounds of bricks from the city walls! In addition, she found that Jericho itself had been completely burned, just as the biblical account records.[13]

An additional archeological recent find has been exciting to me. Those who are familiar with their Bibles recognize the name Caiaphas as a familiar one; he was the Jewish high priest and a Sadducee during the ministry and trial of Jesus. This trial is some of the most dramatic text we find in the New Testament. Caiaphas determines in Matthew 26 that Jesus has committed blasphemy[14] and he turns Jesus over to the Roman governor Pontius Pilate for execution.

In November 1990, while building a new above-ground highway in southeastern Jerusalem, construction workers discovered a burial chamber. Inside the chamber were four caves, containing twelve ossuaries, or bone boxes. The most ornate of these ossuaries contained the bones of a sixty-year-old man, and bore an inscription indicating that this was Caiaphas' ossuary. After much testing on the bone box itself and the bones found inside, archeologists determined that this really was Caiaphas' ossuary and as such, is the first remains found of a person referenced in the Bible. As part of the evidence presented that this was indeed Caiaphas' ossuary, Zvi Greenhut, the Director of the Artifacts Treatment Department of the Israel Antiquities Authority and the person who directed the excavation of the caves states, "When I arrived, I observed that the roof of the cave had collapsed. But even while standing outside, I could see four ossuaries, or bone boxes, in the central chamber of the cave. To an archaeologist, this was a clear indication that this was a Jewish burial cave from the Second Temple period (which is during the time of Caiaphas), because ossuaries were used only in Jewish tombs during this period. Ossuaries were used for what is known as secondary burial.[15]

While many other examples of the historical accuracy of the Bible exist, these are my two favorite examples and they reveal that the Bible actually proves itself to be an historically accurate book.

2. From Genesis to Revelation, the Bible reads as one book.

An incredible unity has been interwoven into the Bible. Although the Bible

---

12. Kathleen M. Kenyon, Excavations at Jericho, 3:110, London, British School of Archaeology in Jerusalem, 1981
13. Joshua 6:24
14. Matthew 26:65
15. Greenhut, Zvi. "Burial Cave of the Caiaphas Family" Biblical Archeology Review, Sept/Oct 1992

is considered to be one book, it is actually a library of sixty-six books! The Bible is complete in its organization and it has a great variety to its literary forms: out of these sixty-six books, we find historical books as well as books of law, wisdom, poetry, prophecy, epistles, and the Gospel. The Bible was written by at least forty different authors over a period of 1,600 years, in thirteen different countries and on three separate continents. It was written in at least three different languages by people in very different professions. While some Christians believe that God dictated the Bible "word for word" in the various languages that the Bible was written and that the authors were simply secretaries who recorded these words, I would think a more precise understanding of the inspiration of Scripture is that God provided the exact thoughts to the human authors, all forty of them, who then wrote it down in words that were familiar to each author utilizing his own vocabulary, education, culture and writing style. This truth is part of what makes the Bible so amazing! Though written over a lengthy period of time, the Bible forms one beautiful temple of truth that does not contradict itself theologically, morally, ethically, doctrinally, scientifically, historically, or in any other way!

3. Did you know that the Bible is the only book in the world that has accurate prophecy?

When we read the prophecies in the Bible, we must simply stand back in amazement! Over 300 precise prophecies about the Lord Jesus Christ can be found in the Old Testament, then are fulfilled in the New Testament. And when a book accurately and repeatedly predicts events well into the future, we can say without hesitation that something special is happening! In fact, the idea that these prophecies were fulfilled "by chance" is an astronomical impossibility.

Here is just one example that I often use when teaching. Nahum is often referred to as a 'minor' prophet, who lived in the seventh century B.C., and preached in a time when the people of Nineveh would not repent. Nineveh, who had destroyed Israel's northern kingdom in 622 B.C.,[16] was overtaken itself by Assyrian forces. In the book of Nahum chapter 3, the prophet wrote 'There will the fire devour you; the sword will cut you off. It will devour you like the locust. Multiply yourselves like the locust; multiply like the grasshopper!'[17] In this prophecy, Nahum said that Nineveh would be damaged by fire. Archeologists unearthed Nineveh in the 1800's

---

16. 2 Kings 17
17. Nahum 3:15

and found a layer of ash over the ruins. According to the Encyclopedia Britannica, 'Nineveh suffered a defeat from which it never recovered. Extensive traces of ash, representing the sack of the city by Babylonians, Scythians, and Medes in 612 BCE, have been found in many parts of the Acropolis.'[18]

4. The Bible is not a book of the month, but the Book of the ages.

No book has ever had as much opposition as the Bible. People for centuries have laughed at it, scorned it, burned it, ridiculed it, and made laws against it. Friedrich Nietzsche, a German philosopher whose work has had a profound influence on Western philosophy and modern intellectual history, concluded near the end of his career that Christianity was "the *one* great curse, the one great intrinsic depravity," and "the one immortal blemish of mankind."[19] His opinion of the Bible was just as unflattering, as he assumed the Bible had no lasting power and would be obsolete within a matter of years. But the Word of God has survived.

The famous French philosopher Voltaire was quoted as saying, 'One hundred years from today the Bible will be a forgotten book.' And yet, fifty years after his death, the new owner of his old home was the president of the Evangelical Society of Geneva, and his home served as a repository for Bibles!

The Bible is as applicable today as it was yesterday and will be tomorrow. The Bible has remained the best-selling book of all time, with over five billion copies printed between 1815 and 2017. The apostle Peter says it best when he writes in 1 Peter, 'All flesh is like grass and all its glory like the flower of grass. The grass withers, and the flower fails, but the word of the Lord remains forever."[20]

The Bible is truly the best book of all time. As we have looked at whether it meets any criteria we might have about whether it is the inspired Word of God and is worthy of our obedience, there should be no question that the Bible is worth our time to read, study and obey. As Paul encourages young Timothy in his ministry, he writes, "Do your best to present yourself to God as one approved, a worker who has no need to be ashamed, rightly handling the word of truth."[21] We would be wise to follow the same advice, to 'rightly handle' the word of truth. So, what are some first steps we should take?

---

18. Mallowan, Max. "Nineveh." Encyclopaedia Britannica. https://www.britannica.com/place/Nineveh-ancient-city-Iraq17. Nahum 3:15

19. Kee, Alistair. Nietzsche Against The Crucified., First Edition. Hymns Ancient & Modern Ltd. 1999
20. 1 Peter 1:24-25
21. 2 Timothy 2:15

First Steps toward Being Obedient to the Bible

There are two initial steps toward being obedient to the Bible. First, we must know God's Word and secondly, we must learn through the proper tools how to obey what we are reading in the Bible.

As I meet with people to help them grow in their walk with the Lord, I often talk about "spiritual disciplines." A spiritual discipline is a practice that we find in Scripture that promotes spiritual growth in the life of a disciple of Jesus. Just as the name indicates, it takes discipline to accomplish these practices well. The spiritual discipline of daily reading the Bible is no different.

The time you spend in God's Word will, in large part, determine how well you are doing in growing to know and be like Jesus. And just like any other discipline, the first key is to get into the habit of doing the discipline daily. It's much like the habit of brushing your teeth! When you were a young child, your parents likely helped you develop the habit of brushing your teeth every day. They emphasized the importance, and just like any well-developed habit, today you probably don't have to think about brushing your teeth. You just do it without even thinking about it! You can develop the same type of habit with Bible reading, just like brushing your teeth. A key to the habit of daily Bible reading can be to find the right place, the right time and the right plan. I like to do my daily Bible reading in a big brown recliner at home, and when I walk by that recliner at other times of the day, I often reflect, 'That's the spot where I read my Bible.'

Developing a routine is your best friend when it comes to building this habit. And just like brushing your teeth, before long reading the Bible each day will become a habit and you will not even have to think about planning to do it! Over time, you can choose to move from reading one chapter a day to something more 'next level.' In the Resources section of this book, you'll find a three-point topical Bible study that you can use to begin doing topical studies. This will help you grow in even greater understanding of God's Word and will make you an 'expert' in certain topics in a very short time!

After the initial step of just regularly reading your Bible, the next step in finding biblical obedience is beginning to obey what God is teaching you through your time investment in His word. Jesus tells us, "If you love me, you will keep my commandments."[22] Recall the passage in James I mentioned before:

> "But be doers of the word, and not hearers only, deceiving yourselves. For if anyone is a hearer of the word and not a doer, he is like a man who looks intently at his natural face in a mirror. For he looks at himself and goes away and at once forgets what he was like.[23]

As we encounter God's Word in our daily time, we surely don't want to be like the person who looks in a mirror, then goes away and forgets what he looks like! As we invest time with God, He will tell us to do certain actions, and we then must be obedient to do them. View this from a parenting perspective: you recall my story about my son and the dishwasher. As his father, I will be happy when I observe that he does what I tell him to do. God is only happy when we do the same. Jesus tells us in John 13 that *"Now that you know these things, you will be blessed if you do them."*[24]

A great practical way to become a doer of the Word is to always write out an action step as a result of your reading, studying or reflecting on God's Word. Develop the habit of writing down exactly what you intend to do to be obedient to what you have read. This may be in a journal you keep with you as you invest time with God in his Word, or you might use a computer or smart phone. This action step should be (1) personal (involving you), (2) practical (something you can do), and (3) provable (with a deadline)! Every action step will involve either your relationship to God, your relationship to others, or your personal character.

---

22. John 14:15
23. James 1:22-24
24. John 13:17

Discussion Questions

Self-Reflection Questions

1. As you read the historical and biblical 'proofs' for the reliability of the Bible, how does that change your perception of God's Word as a reliable book?

2. Based on your experience, what have you found regarding scripture and its reliability, authority, relevance, and impact on your life?

3. What has God already shown you in His Word that you want to begin to change or do, out of obedience and the desire to please Him?

4. What obstacles keep you from the spiritual discipline of reading God's Word daily? What action steps could you take to begin developing a habit of reading God's Word daily?

Group Discussion Questions

5. Do you have any question about whether the Bible is the inspired Word of God? If so, share one of those concerns.

6. Have you used a journal as part of your daily reading of God's word? If so, how has writing your thoughts, prayers or responses helped you in obeying Scripture?

7. What are some practices you regularly use for connecting with God through Scripture?

8. How do you think writing action steps as mentioned in this chapter might help you? What help do you need from others within this group to encourage and hold you accountable to accomplish the action steps God gives you?

Chapter 5

The Fourth Mark of a Disciple of Jesus

Fruitful for Christ

I love growing trees in my back yard! We so enjoy the shade of their leafy branches on summer days, and what beauty they bring to our local landscape.

But I do have a rule as it relates to the trees I plant in my back yard: they must be some type of fruit tree. If I am going to invest the effort into watering and caring for a young tree, I want a return for my time investment! I also love picking freshly ripened fruit from the trees and enjoying the fruit with my family. One of my backyard fruit trees is a Bartlett pear tree. If you live in the U.S. or Canada, I'll bet you have tasted a Bartlett pear, as 80% of all pears grown in the U.S. are of the Bartlett variety. The Bartlett pears are so delicious and also quite nutritious.

My Bartlett pear tree has an interesting history. When I bought it to plant in my back yard, it started out with very humble beginnings. If you had seen the tree when we planted it soon after we first moved into our home, you wouldn't have thought that it was going to amount to much! Just a scraggly little $20 Home Depot tree, as skinny and small as it could be. When I bought it, I was a little fearful that it might not survive the first of its Colorado winters.

Not only did it make it through the first winter, the spindly little tree grew quickly and seemed to thrive in the place where I had planted it. To our surprise, at the end of the third summer, the pear tree actually began to *grow pears!* And after the fourth summer, we *really* began to enjoy a plentiful pear harvest! I don't know if I planted it in just the right place in our yard, or if we just got lucky, but when the conditions are right, it now produces a huge bounty of pears!

Currently, our family of five can't eat all the pears we get from this tree. We end up giving away pears to neighbors, friends, and anyone else we can find who likes to eat pears. Last summer, we had so many pears that we had to resign ourselves to allowing some of the pears to fall to the ground uneaten. Harvesting the pears and getting them to people who want to take them has nearly become a part-time job!

The Fourth Mark of a Disciple of Jesus is *that a disciple of Jesus is fruitful for Christ*. Jesus states this expectation clearly in Matthew 7:

> "You will recognize them by their fruits. Are grapes gathered from thorn bushes, or figs from thistles? So, every healthy tree bears good fruit, but the diseased tree bears bad fruit. A healthy tree cannot bear bad fruit, nor can a diseased tree bear good fruit. Every tree that does not bear good fruit is cut down and thrown into the fire. Thus you will recognize them by their fruits."[1]

Just like my Bartlett pear tree--which is getting the right amount of sun and water and was apparently planted in just the right spot—is bearing fruit because it is healthy and is getting all that it needs to grow and produce fruit.

Disciples of Jesus—those who have a relationship with Jesus and are being fed through God's Word and time with Him in prayer—cannot help but produce good fruit. Let's look at what good spiritual fruit looks like and what conditions are necessary to produce it.

As we examine this Mark of a disciple, I'd like for us to think in three directions. First, what is biblical fruit? Because there are many different definitions and descriptions of the meaning of this term among Christians, I'd like to clarify the definition so we are all on the same page. Secondly, we will look at how we can become "fruit bearers." And finally, I'd love to offer a personal challenge to you about bearing fruit. As believers, of course we all want to be Christians who are bearing fruit, but what does that look like biblically? As we spend time closely connected to Jesus, biblical fruit is simply the outward manifestation of our relationship with Jesus. A disciple of Jesus's life should view his or her own life as a fruit-bearing life.

There are least four ways that I've seen that spiritual fruit manifests itself in our lives as we walk with Jesus.

---

1. Matthew 7:16-20

1. The Way We Talk

The manifestation of 'a good tree producing good fruit' almost immediately shows itself through the way a Christian speaks. Jesus stated it best:

"For no good tree bears bad fruit, nor again does a bad tree bear good fruit, for each tree is known by its own fruit. For figs are not gathered from thornbushes, nor are grapes picked from a bramble bush. The good person out of the good treasure of his heart produces good, and the evil person out of his evil treasure produces evil, for out of the abundance of the heart his mouth speaks."[2]

I cannot begin to describe how true the last part of this verse is: "for out of the abundance of the heart his mouth speaks." What is inside the heart, either an abiding love and dependence on Jesus or a fleshly desire to please oneself, really does come out through the way that we speak. In times that I am not connected well to Jesus, I am more prone to lash out at my children or colleagues—but when I am well-connected with Jesus, that temptation is not as prevalent. Good treasure stored up in the heart produces God-honoring speech.

2. The Way We Worship

We worship Jesus because of what He did for us on the cross: taking our place for the punishment we deserve. As we read in Hebrews 13, "Through him then let us continually offer up a sacrifice of praise to God, that is, the fruit of lips that acknowledge his name."[3] We can bear fruit with our lips by praising God! The biblical writer is using the same terminology we see in the Old Testament when a sacrifice was offered to placate God. For example, as Hosea is pleading with the Israelites to return to God, he writes (in Hosea 14), "Take with you words and return to the LORD; say to him, "Take away all iniquity; accept what is good, and we will pay with bulls the vows of our lips."[4] With Christ's substitutionary sacrifice on the cross, we no longer have to 'pay with bulls;' instead, we now can offer a thank offering to God as we praise Him with our lips. When we offer thankful acknowledgment to God, our lips bear fruit as we continually --throughout the course our days—praise and thank the Lord.

---

2. Luke 6:43-45
3. Hebrews 13:15
4. Hosea 14:2

3. Loving People and Seeing People Coming to Christ

One of the most obvious ways that we bear fruit is how the manifestation of the Gospel in our lives produces new believers. Disciples of Jesus have a clear testimony of what God has done in their lives and continually pursue opportunities to share the Gospel with others. In my ministry, I often say to people that at the very least, every Christian should be able to share their testimony of how they came to know Jesus, and to share a simple Gospel presentation. As mentioned previously in this book, disciples of Jesus want to share the Gospel, knowing what Jesus has done in their lives. I have found that a disciple can't help but share what God has done in his life. A disciple should take the attitude of Jesus when He said, "My food is to do the will of him who sent me and to accomplish his work. Do you not say, 'There are yet four months, then comes the harvest'? Look, I tell you, lift up your eyes, and see that the fields are white for harvest. Already the one who reaps is receiving wages and gathering fruit for eternal life, so that sower and reaper may rejoice together.[5] We are certainly bearing fruit 'for eternal life' as we share the reason for the hope we have in Jesus. This fruitfulness of winning others to Christ is a clear evidence of someone who is abiding closely to Jesus.

4. Fruit of the Spirit

We cannot discount the role that the Holy Spirit plays in the life of a disciple of Jesus. Our first encounter with the Holy Spirit comes as He initially convicts us of sin.[6] As we repent, confess our sins and receive the gift of salvation, the Holy Spirit performs a work of regeneration, which allows us to become sensitive to the spiritual things of God.[7] Fruit is then produced in the life of the disciple of Jesus who has been baptized by the Holy Spirit.[8] The apostle Paul lays this out for us in Galatians, "But I say, walk by the Spirit, and you will not gratify the desires of the flesh. For the desires of the flesh are against the Spirit, and the desires of the Spirit are against the flesh, for these are opposed to each other, to keep you from doing the things you want to do... But the fruit of the Spirit is love, joy, peace, patience, kindness, goodness, faithfulness, gentleness, self-control; against such things there is no law. And those who belong to Christ Jesus have crucified the

---

5. John 4:34-36
6. John 16:8-11
7. John 3:1-16; Acts 2:38
8. Acts 2:1-4

flesh with its passions and desires."[9] The Christian connected to Jesus should see these nine attributes growing more prevalent in their lives. Spiritual fruit will reveal itself in our lives as our character and outlook begin to change! As we invest in time with Jesus and get to know Him better, His thoughts will become our thoughts and His purpose will become our purpose, and we will become like Jesus. The Greek word Paul uses in this passage for the word fruit refers to a natural product of a living thing, just like a pear tree must produce pears. There is simply no way for a healthy fruit tree to not bear fruit!

The obvious next question, then, has to be, 'How do we become productive bearers of spiritual fruit as disciples of Jesus?' To answer this question, we start by looking at what Jesus says about this in John 15 as He gives us a clear answer to this question. In a lengthy teaching session that spans from John 13 through chapter 17, Jesus tells us that we bear fruit as we abide in Him. Let's take a close look at this chapter to discern what Jesus is saying about bearing fruit.

Jesus begins this lesson by stating, "I am the true vine, and my Father is the vinedresser." Already we see different roles for Jesus and for God the Father: Jesus is the vine, but God is the vinedresser. A vinedresser is someone whose profession is to continually prune and care for the vines. As we'll see in a minute, we have a role in the story as well: the branches. Jesus continues, "Every branch in me that does not bear fruit he takes away, and every branch that does bear fruit he prunes, that it may bear more fruit." So, God is very actively involved in our fruit-bearing. As we are attached to the vine, He is pruning us and helping us bear more fruit. If you have ever grown a fruit tree, you know that it does help the tree to bear more fruit when you prune it!

Many times, I find that God's pruning in my relationship with Jesus involves God disciplining me for a wrong thought pattern or belief that does not honor Him. The author of Hebrews must have experienced something similar, as he wrote, "For the moment all discipline seems painful rather than pleasant, but later it yields the peaceful fruit of righteousness to those who have been trained by it."[10]

"Abide in me, and I in you," Jesus continues, with an interesting choice in words. The English word 'abide' is the Greek word meno, which means 'to remain in' or 'to stay in.' The implication I get from this is that Jesus wants us to become like Him. What is the key to bearing fruit? To become more like Jesus, and Jesus says

---

9. Galatians 5:16-24
10. Hebrews 12:11

as much in the following verse: "As the branch cannot bear fruit by itself, unless it abides in the vine, neither can you, unless you abide in me. I am the vine; you are the branches. Whoever abides in me and I in him, he it is that bears much fruit, for apart from me you can do nothing."[11] Jesus must be in the center of our lives and we must depend on Him for everything in order to bear fruit. We cannot expect to bear fruit on our own! This is one of the biggest errors I think most Christians make: to think you are going to be a 'Sunday-only' Christian, then forget about Jesus for the rest of the week and still bear fruit is a clear error of judgment.

I have chosen to present the Six Marks of a Disciple in the order I have presented them for an important reason. Only after we determine who we are in Christ—fully identifying with Him and doing a self-check on our love and dedication for Jesus—does He then prepare us for the Mark of being fruitful for Christ. We must analyze how we are doing in the first two Marks before moving on. I am convinced that the true disciples of Jesus, those who love him to such a degree that they are willing to deny themselves, abandon everything they have for Jesus, and love Jesus with a deep desire to obey Him, to honor Him, to serve Him, and to proclaim Him, do not have to try very hard to bear fruit because, at that stage in their walk with Jesus, they actually cannot help but bear fruit! They cannot help to bear fruit any more than my healthy pear tree cannot help producing pears. The tree simply does what God made it to do! Jesus addresses this in Mark 4, as He is explaining the Parable of the Sower, "But those that were sown on the good soil are the ones who hear the Word and accept it and bear fruit, thirtyfold and sixtyfold and a hundredfold." A three-step process for those whose 'soil' or relationship with Jesus is good: (1) hear the Word, (2) accept it and (3) bear fruit.

There is more to the story of my Bartlett pear tree! I planted the tree in my back yard in the summer of 2004 when it was just a skinny $20 tree. In early 2007, we brought a new dog into our family: our Wheaten Terrier named Boaz, who has been an overwhelming blessing to our family except for this one occasion! In the summer of 2007, just as our pear tree was beginning to produce pears, Boaz felt it necessary to chew on the trunk of my beloved pear tree. By the time we noticed what he was doing, Boaz had chewed almost halfway through the trunk! If there was ever a time that I wanted to take him right back where he came from, it was when I first found out what he had done to my pear tree! Instead, I put tree repair

---

11. John 15:1-5

tape on the trunk and allowed Boaz to stay in this family, and over the course of the next couple of years, the tree trunk healed--albeit with a permanent "Boaz-inflicted" scar on the trunk!

As I present this material to you, it is my earnest prayer that Jesus would begin to show you the idols and distractions that are coming between you and Jesus, and that may be preventing you from bearing fruit for Him. Maybe the source is an unresolved sin that you need to address, or maybe a selfish attitude of 'me first' that is keeping you from abiding well in Him. Or perhaps, just like my pear tree which took a serious hit to its ability to survive, you may feel like Jesus could never use you to bear fruit because of what you've done or what has occurred in your past. Jesus came to 'bind up the brokenhearted, to proclaim liberty to the captives, and the opening of the prison to those who are bound.'[12] This passage from Isaiah has been very impactful for me as I've learned its meaning: that Jesus has come to 'put a dressing on to heal the bleeding and damaged heart.' Just as I put tape on the trunk of my tree and it gradually healed, and is now bearing fruit, Jesus wants to heal you from your broken and damaged heart as well. And He wants then to use you to bear much fruit. In John 15 Jesus says, "By this my Father is glorified, that you bear much fruit and so prove to be my disciples."[13] The mark of a disciple is to bear much fruit, and, in the process, we bring glory to God.

First Steps to Bearing Spiritual Fruit

Here are some first steps you can take to begin bearing fruit for God. I encourage you to pray through each of these three steps, ask God for help in areas that you need help, and ask someone in your life to hold you accountable to the action items you develop to see forward progress in these areas.

1. Allow Jesus full reign in your life

Invest some time in assessing where you are now in your relationship with Jesus. What areas are you keeping from Him and not allowing Him to access? In his final admonitions to the Corinthian Church, Paul calls for this 'self-check' of their lives in Christ, and it is good counsel for us as well: "Examine yourselves, to see whether you are in the faith. Test yourselves. Or do you not realize this about yourselves,

---

12. Isaiah 61:1
13. John 15:8

that Jesus Christ is in you?—unless indeed you fail to meet the test!"[14]

As we assess the place of honor that Jesus holds in our lives and because we've surrendered our lives to Jesus and now belong to Him who has been raised from the dead, as Paul writes, "we may now bear fruit for God."[15]

2. Stay humble to bear fruit

"Bear fruit in keeping with repentance,"[16] John the Baptist admonished the Pharisees and Sadducees as they were hanging around the place where Jesus was to be baptized. The Greek word for *repent* means "to change one's mind." When John told them to produce fruit in keeping with repentance, he was admonishing them to change their minds and admit that they desperately needed Jesus and could not save themselves. For us as well, this is such an important concept. We must recognize that we cannot bear fruit by our own power; we also need a changed heart and a dependence on Jesus. Invest some time to assess this in your own life.

3. Make Yourself Available

God is always looking for faithful men and women to accomplish His will. In 2 Chronicles we read, 'For the eyes of the LORD range throughout the earth to strengthen those whose hearts are fully committed to him.'[17] As you ask God to use you in whatever way He sees fit to bear fruit, you may be surprised at how well He can use someone who is fully committed to Him! He is looking for people like that! Not only will God give you a fruit-bearing work to do, but He will strengthen your heart as He gives you the task.

A suggestion: try a number of different opportunities to see where you are gifted, and which areas might be a good match for you. When assessing one's spiritual gifts for example, there are not only spiritual gifts tests (and if you haven't ever taken one of these tests, I highly recommend them)[18], but there are also ways to test for spiritual gifts through experiences you've had. As you have more opportunities and experiences in ministry, you can assess which of the opportunities God has blessed

---

14. 2 Corinthians 13:5
15. Romans 7:4
16. Matthew 3:8
17. 2 Chronicles 16:9, New International Version
18. While there are many good spiritual gifts tests available, I would recommend two: For an initial look at your spiritual gifts, try the free online test at https://spiritualgiftstest.com/. For a more in-depth look, the Everybody Has A Part by Ministry Tool Resource Center is excellent. They have different variations that examine 7, 15 or 20 gifts. For about $20 USD, you can self-administer any of the tests, and they include resources for understanding your gift better, how to use the findings, and insights about your gift. The shortest version (35 questions) that assesses 7 gifts is available free on their website at https://mintools-store.com/products/spiritual-gifts-tests.

and you've see where fruit was borne.[19] For example, if you were asked to teach a lesson in your Sunday School class, and people come up to you afterword and tell you how much they learned from your teaching, you may have the spiritual gift of teaching. God is asking today, as He did in Isaiah's times, "Whom shall I send, and who will go for us?" He is looking for people who will reply, "Here I am! Send me."[20] And as we've seen throughout this book, we are all called to find places to find involvement in God's Kingdom work. None of us is exempt!

Discussion Questions

Self-Reflection Questions

1. Given the definitions in this chapter as to what biblical fruit is in our lives, how are you doing at becoming a good fruit bearer?

2. In John 4, Jesus says, "Already the one who reaps is receiving wages and gathering fruit for eternal life, so that sower and reaper may rejoice together." Are there people in your life whom you'd like to see come into relationship with Jesus, so that you could 'gather that fruit?' If so, who are they?

---

19. In the Resources section at the end of this book, I have included a list of Spiritual Gifts and a brief explanation of each gift.
20. Isaiah 6:8

3. If it is true that a real disciple of Jesus does not have to try very hard to bear fruit, what reflections can you draw from your own life?

4. You were challenged in this chapter to look at obstacles that may in in your way toward bearing fruit. What idols and unresolved sin do you think might be standing between you and Jesus?

Group Discussion Questions

1. Hebrews 12 states, "For the moment all discipline seems painful rather than pleasant, but later it yields the peaceful fruit of righteousness to those who have been trained by it." What role have you seen the discipline of God play in your walk with Jesus, and how has it produced good fruit in your life as you have been trained by it?

2. As you desire to abide in Christ, knowing that you demonstrate that you are a disciple of Jesus as you bear much fruit, what areas of change or growth would you like this group to help you with and hold you accountable for in your walk with Jesus?

3. What spiritual fruit would you like to begin seeking, praying for, and practicing in your life? What might this look like practically for you?

4. As you read through the list of the Fruit of the Spirit in Galatians 5, how do you fare in seeing these nine attributes growing in your life? Which of these would you like to work on next?

Chapter 6

The Fifth Mark of a Disciple of Jesus

Filled with Love for Others

I have thoroughly enjoyed growing up and currently living in Colorado. This beautiful state affords those who live here many benefits, especially if you enjoy the great outdoors! For me, growing up in Colorado meant that I would become a big fan of this state's major sport teams. My dad had season tickets for the Denver Broncos, our NFL football team, and shared season tickets with a friend for the Denver Nuggets, our NBA basketball team.

During the years that I was a child, Colorado only had minor league baseball teams. Our team was the Denver Bears, later known as the Denver Zephyrs. Major League Baseball (MLB) didn't come to Denver until 1993, with the expansion Colorado Rockies starting play that year. Since we didn't have a MLB team until I had grown up and moved out of my parents' house, I didn't really follow baseball closely until the 2007 season when the Rockies won 21 out of their last 22 games to reach the World Series for the first time in their history! Before this 2007 'miracle' season, they had only been to the playoffs once, and I just happened to catch the first game that started the winning streak on TV because I was home with a bad cold. The Rockies won that game, so I decided to watch the next game—and they won again. And every day I tuned in to a game, and they would win every time I watched them, which began to cement in me a newfound interest in this team. I began to learn about the players, their stories and personalities, and began to connect with the players.

The Rockies had to continue their winning streak in order to make the playoffs and it all came down to the 162nd game of the season, which was also their last game of the season. The Rockies had to win that game, and the San Diego Padres had to lose their game against the Milwaukee Brewers in order for the Rockies and Padres to end the season with an identical record, which meant they would play in a 163rd game of the year, a one-game playoff! A friend of mine with tickets to the final game of the year invited me to go with him to the game.

As we watched the game unfold that day, we all had our eyes also on the scoreboard that sits in right field of Coors Field, the home of the Rockies. Because the Padres-Brewers game had started before the Rockies game and the Padres had to lose, we were watching that scoreboard as much as we were watching the game at Coors Field! This created a funny dynamic during the game, because when the scoreboard operator would change the score of the Padres game and show that the Brewers had scored, there were loud cheers that had nothing to do with the Rockies game! After we learned that the Brewers had defeated the Padres, all we needed now was for the Rockies to win their game. During parts of the 8th and 9th innings as the Rockies made the hits and the plays that they needed to win their game, my friend and I would high-five and cheer with people we had never met before. This is one of the great benefits to cities and states for having professional sports teams: these games bring the people of the city together in ways very few events can. At that moment, we weren't from different ethnic backgrounds or parts of the city, we were all just Colorado Rockies fans, all so very proud of our team and our city! As the Rockies pitcher made a crucial pick up of the ball and threw to first base for the final out to secure the Rockies win, a Hispanic man standing two rows behind me leaped over the row between us and hugged me and my friend in celebration! We all celebrated and whooped it up for probably 15 minutes after the game was over. This singular event was truly one of the best sports experiences of my life!

I often think of that experience when pondering the Fifth Mark of a Disciple of Jesus: the deep love we must have for each other as Christians, and as I'll write about later in this chapter, a deep love and concern for all mankind. If I could feel this camaraderie, this love for people I had never met before, over an event that was so temporal, how much more should I love those whom I call brothers and sisters in Christ?

Not only is the committed disciple preoccupied with his Lord's glory, but he also is filled with God's love. A distinguishing mark of being a follower of Christ is a deep, sincere love for brothers and sisters in Christ. Perhaps this distinguishing mark of the committed Christian is the most significant of all in terms of practical living because we tend to be around people all the time!

As we'll see in our main passage of Scripture found in the book of John, being filled with love for brothers and sisters in Christ is quite clearly a mark of a disciple. Being a follower of Christ means carrying a real, deep and sincere love for brothers and sisters in Christ. There is no better passage for our focus than John 13, as we see Jesus with His disciples. He is nearing the end of His earthly ministry, and is spending his last evening the disciples on the night before He will be crucified. Jesus chooses this opportunity to wash the disciples' feet, and to give them the last of His instructions. If any of us could know when we were dying and leaving this earth, the final instructions we would give to those we love the most would be so important. We wouldn't waste time on "fluff," but would get right to the point, talking about deeply important and significant matters. Jesus takes exactly this approach in the last chapters of the book of John. "A new commandment I give to you," Jesus states, "that you love one another: just as I have loved you, you also are to love one another. By this all people will know that you are my disciples, if you have love for one another."[1]

This new commandment that Jesus gives to his disciples is contrasted against the 'old commandment' that we discussed in Chapter 3:

> 'You shall love the Lord your God with all your heart and with all your soul and with all your mind. This is the great and first commandment. And a second is like it: You shall love your neighbor as yourself.'[2]

So, very near the end of His earthly ministry, Jesus gives another command to be obeyed by those who follow Him. In this new command, Jesus shows his concern for how those who follow Jesus treat each other, and how, then, that interaction reflects their commitment to Christ.

---

1. John 13:34-35
2. Matthew 22:37-39

This commandment stands out from the old commandment in a couple of important ways. First, the new commandment focuses on the love we each receive from Christ. The love Jesus gives becomes the very source of Christian love. Secondly, the new commandment is a community-building commandment within the bond of believers. As Christ's followers demonstrate love for one another, they also demonstrate and express the love they receive from Christ. Let's explore three main parts of these verses in John 13 at a deeper level.

This passage begins with Jesus calling us to love one another. Because of the context in which Jesus spoke this command to His disciples, His desire and command is for believers to love other believers. Because we are called by Jesus to love one another in the same way that He has loved us, showing the rest of the world that we are His disciples, we had better do it intentionally well!

Additional study on this topic reveals that the apostle John was deeply impacted by this new commandment. In fact, John makes this new commandment a repetitive talking point in his own letters to congregations across Asia Minor (now Turkey) on at least six occasions in 1 John. This was something that stuck with John even after Jesus had ascended into heaven and John continued his ministry. Look at these examples from I John:

> *Whoever says he is in the light and hates his brother is still in darkness. Whoever loves his brother abides in the light, and in him there is no cause for stumbling.*[3]

> *For this is the message that you have heard from the beginning, that we should love one another.*[4]

> *We know that we have passed out of death into life, because we love the brothers. Whoever does not love abides in death. Everyone who hates his brother is a murderer, and you know that no murderer has eternal life abiding in him.*[5]

> *And this is his commandment, that we believe in the name of his Son Jesus Christ and love one another, just as he has commanded us. Whoever keeps his commandments abides in God, and God in him. And by this we know that he abides in us, by the Spirit whom he has given us.*[6]

---

3. 1 John 2:9-10
4. 1 John 3:11
5. 1 John 3:14-15
6. 1 John 3:23-24

Beloved, let us love one another, for love is from God, and whoever loves has been born of God and knows God. Anyone who does not love does not know God, because God is love.[7]

If anyone says, "I love God," and hates his brother, he is a liar; for he who does not love his brother whom he has seen cannot love God whom he has not seen. And this commandment we have from him: whoever loves God must also love his brother.[8]

Clearly this 'new commandment' stuck with John. In fact, none of the other three gospel books in the New Testament record Jesus saying this 'new commandment.' Could it have been that John, named as the disciple that Jesus loved, heard and took note of this commandment when the others did not? We will never know in this life, but clearly John was deeply impressed by the command for Christians to have a deep love for other Christians. John emphasizes a few aspects of this love in the passages of 1 John: First, Jesus commanded us to love each other and whoever keeps the commands of Jesus has God living in him.

Also, I am struck by how many times John says, 'If you hate your brother, you do not know God and you are a liar.' Why did John choose to call this person a liar? Simply put, if you say you love Jesus and hate your brother or sister, you are only saying you love God (remember the title of this book!). In reality, you do not love God. You cannot carry both emotions in place at the same time.

In order to love our brothers and sisters in the way we should, John offers a blueprint for how that love should be lived. Remember Jesus' words in John 13:34? "Just as I have loved you," Jesus says, "you also are to love one another." Talk about Jesus raising the bar! In the same ways that Jesus loved us, we're supposed to love one another? I don't know about you, but I don't think I'm going to be able to love anyone in the same way Jesus loves me! Jesus knows that to be true, but it's clear that He wants to set the bar high.

So, how can this command be accomplished? While the topic of how much Jesus loves us was covered extensively in Chapter 2, let's look at what loving others in the way Jesus loves us would look like.

First, it would be an unconditional love. We read in Romans 5 about how unconditional God's love for us is, as Paul writes, "But God shows his love for us in

---

7. 1 John 4:7-8
8. 1 John 4:20-21

that while we were still sinners, Christ died for us.[9] So perhaps we could work on loving our brothers and sisters in Christ in such a way that there would be fewer conditions, understanding that we are all sinners saved by grace and we all need each other's love to get through life.

This love would also be a sacrificial love—in much the same way that 'he made him to be sin who knew no sin, so that in him we might become the righteousness of God.'[10] We could go out of our way to sacrifice more for each other, especially if a brother or sister had done something to us that we didn't like or appreciate. We see evidence of this active kind of love in the book of Acts, where 'all who believed were together and had all things in common.'[11]

What happened to this type of togetherness and love in the Christian church? To still love our brothers and sisters despite unfavorable circumstances would be at least somewhat like what Jesus did for us. He had no sin himself, but He took it on for us so that we could cross the bridge from death to life. And certainly, ours would be a love full of forgiveness! Forgiveness would permeate our relationships with each other. In my favorite verse in this regard, Paul writes to the Ephesian church to "Be kind to one another, tenderhearted, forgiving one another, as God in Christ forgave you."[12] We all know that if our interactions with fellow believers were kind, tenderhearted and forgiving, these interactions would be a lot better!

Finally, this love for our fellow believers would have what I call a *1 Corinthians 13* love. We all know the famous passage where Paul writes,

> "Love is patient and kind; love does not envy or boast; it is not arrogant or rude. It does not insist on its own way; it is not irritable or resentful; it does not rejoice at wrongdoing, but rejoices with the truth. Love bears all things, believes all things, hopes all things, endures all things.[13]

A Bible teacher I heard once told the class that, as a way to test how you are doing exhibiting "1 Corinthians 13 love," replace the word 'love' in this passage with your first name. So, for me, it would read 'Mike is patient and kind; Mike does not envy or boast....'

Go ahead and try it now with your first name.

How did you do? Do the statements accurately describe the way you love others?

---

9. Romans 5:8
10. 2 Corinthians 5:21
11. Acts 2:44
12. Ephesians 4:32
13. 1 Corinthians 13:4-7

Imagine now what our churches would look if we could love each other in this way! The question then has to be asked: Why don't we see this type of love in our churches more often? It's a complicated answer, but certainly too few of us are taking Jesus' command to 'love one another as Jesus loves us' seriously. And it doesn't take much more than a rudimentary internet search to see some of the horror stories of reasons people are leaving churches, and instances of brothers and sisters in Christ *not* loving each other in ways that would show obedience to the command we have been studying in this chapter.

If you have been around churches for any significant amount of time, you have probably seen and experienced this 'non-love' many believers have for their fellow Christians. Having a conflict with another believer, for example, is not a good reason to leave a church!

So, what's the answer? A deep and abiding love for Jesus, which I wrote about in the last chapter, is the answer—allowing the vine (Jesus) to nourish the branch (us.) Paul hits the nail on the head when he writes in Romans that "God's love has been poured into our hearts through the Holy Spirit who has been given to us."[14] The prerequisite for loving our brothers and sisters in Christ in this loving way is a relationship with God where we've surrendered our lives to Christ, we have the Holy Spirit living in us and, through that relationship, we bear fruit through our relationships with other Christians.

The final piece to answer the question of why all of this is important is found in John 13:35, as Jesus says, "By this all people will know that you are my disciples, if you have love for one another." As is the case with most of the Marks of a Disciple, if it is true that all people will know that we are His disciples by the way we love one another, the opposite would be true as well. If we don't love each other well, it reflects negatively on what others think of our Christian witness. Unfortunately, the world does have a negative attitude about the church. Often in today's world, when people hear that we are Christians, they are not reminded of this type of self-sacrificing love within the church. Instead, they would describe us using words like "stingy," "rule keepers," or "judgmental." While that judgment may not be fair and may not represent you personally, it is still our responsibility to change what the world thinks of us as Christians.

Think of what an attractional force the church would be to enter into if we

---

14. Romans 5:5

really loved each other well. I think all people, regardless of their previous religious experience, are looking for communities to participate in who love each other well. They want an experience that is similar to my Colorado Rockies story, where I accepted everyone around me, regardless of race, color, religion, or age. We were all just Rockies fans! If that love that we have from Christ would flow over into the world, knowing that we're all humans and Jesus paid the price for us all, we could become known as people who loved others well.

Even though the secular world does not seem to need Jesus or want to know about Him, we know from Scripture that every one of us has a God-shaped hole in our hearts that only He can fill. And we know that Jesus has commanded all of us to preach the Gospel[15] and has given all of us non-Christians within our spheres of influence, whether our neighborhoods, families or workplaces. As I read Jesus' 'new commandment,' I discern that we have two platforms available to us for the Gospel when we do this well in our churches, as illustrated so well by the apostle Paul in 2 Corinthians 2. Paul writes,

> "But thanks be to God, who in Christ always leads us in triumphal procession, and through us spreads the fragrance of the knowledge of him everywhere. For we are the aroma of Christ to God among those who are being saved and among those who are perishing, to one a fragrance from death to death, to the other a fragrance from life to life."[16]

Paul's choice of words here is so fantastic! I can still remember the fragrance of my mother's cooking, especially the lasagna that she would make every year for my birthday. Just the thought of that wonderful scent brings back a flood of good thoughts and memories as I recall waiting impatiently to taste the first delicious bite. The first platform we have with those around us is to be the fragrance or arome of Christ, both to those being saved and those perishing. What aroma are we spreading among these people? Is it a sweet and inviting aroma? Do they know we are disciples of Jesus by the way that we love each other well? The second platform is similar to the first. As we love each other as Christ loves us, my encouragement is for all of us to love everyone we meet in the way Christ loves us!

As we are receiving life from abiding in Christ, let's give that sweet aroma of true life in Christ to all we meet!

---

15. Mark 16:15
16. 2 Corinthians 2:14-16

First Steps toward Loving Our Brothers and Sisters Well

This is such a powerful Mark of a disciple of Jesus, and I believe that we all would love to do this well. The first step I believe you can personally take is to assess troubled relationships you may have with a brother or sister in Christ. Ask yourself a few questions about that relationship:

> Why is this relationship troubled?
>
> What am I bringing to the relationship that is adding to the trouble?
>
> Do I need to 'take the log out of my own eye'[17] first before asking them to do the same?

The next step would be to involve other believers involved if there is still trouble in a relationship. Many times, a third party can really help to discern what is going on. Finally, as you see potential trouble with relationships with believers, remember Jesus' command to do your utmost to be the peacemaker in the relationship.

Discussion Questions

Self-Reflection Questions

1. Do you feel like you have a good sense of how much Jesus loves you? Are you living daily in that reality?

---

17. Matthew 7:4-5

2. How hard is it for you to love other Christians as Jesus has loved you? What are your 'sticking points' for doing that well?

3. How did you do with replacing your name with 'love' in the 1 Corinthians passage? If that brought up areas of needed growth in your ability to love, what commitments do you want to make now before God to turn the tide in this area of your life?

4. Do you think it is possible for us as humans to love with a sacrificial and unconditional love? If so, what kind of environment would needed to do this with your brothers and sisters in Christ?

Group Discussion Questions

5. As you read the six passages from 1 John about God's love living in us, and us loving our Christian brothers and sisters well, how does that challenge you in your own love for other Christians?

6. If a non-Christian came into your study group, what aroma would they get from their observations of you all? The sweet scent of Christ or a smell of contention?

7. What needs to change within your group to ensure the sweet smell of Christ? What issues need to be faced, addressed, and pre-determined policies put in place so that conflict doesn't begin to smell foul?

8. Francis Schaeffer wrote a book called *The Mark of the Christian*. He states in his book about Jesus' requirement for us to love for our brothers and sisters in Christ,

    'The point is that it is possible to be a Christian without showing this mark, but if we expect non-Christians to know that we are Christians, we must show the mark.'[18]

    Discuss what impact you think it would have if we were to 'have love for one another' in our evangelistic efforts.

---

18. Schaeffer, Francis. The Mark of a Christian., 2nd Edition, Intervarsity Press

Chapter 7

The Sixth Mark of a Disciple of Jesus

Dying to Self

For over twenty years, I have had a longstanding desire and heart to impact China for Christ. This desire has taken various forms of ministry involvement over that time, including ministry to international students who have come to the United States from China, serving the growth and development of the church in rural China through Bible distribution, theological training and church building, and most recently, reaching unreached people groups in China through Bible translation. As part of my involvement in China, I have become a Chinese history and culture buff, which has led to the writing and publication of my first book, The Chinese Puzzle, now in its second edition. Through my research about missionary history in China for that book, I became very interested in the lives of early missionaries to China, their motivations for going to China and the ways that God used their surrender to and service for the Gospel in China.

One of the key individuals whom I really enjoyed learning about was Charles Thomas Studd, better known as C.T. Studd. He was a man who knew God's will for his life and most definitely followed it. Born in England in 1860, Studd was one of three sons of a wealthy retired trader, Edward Studd, who had made a fortune in India. After a dramatic conversion experience, he gave up his previous life of leisure to use his fortune toward saving souls in England.

By the time he was sixteen, Studd had become an expert cricket player and would become one of England's finest cricket players. And at nineteen, he was the captain of his cricket team at Eton College. At about this time in his life, a preacher who was visiting the Studd household for meetings with his father caught this young man on his way to play cricket. Shortly after that meeting, Studd accepted Christ as his Savior, but another six years would pass before he would fully surrender his life to Jesus. After a serious illness of one of his brothers, he went to hear the American pastor D.L. Moody, who confronted Studd with the question, "What is all the fame and flattery worth ... when a man comes to face eternity?" Young C.T. admitted to Pastor Moody that since accepting Christ six years earlier, he had been in "an unhappy backslidden state" and knew that "cricket would not last, and honor would not last, and nothing in this world would last, but it was worthwhile living for the world to come."[1]

After his newfound surrender to Christ, Studd began witnessing to friends and cricket teammates. As a part of his new ministry, in early 1884 he attended a meeting where he heard for the first time about the needs of the unreached in China. His heart was heavily burdened by what he heard, and long after the evening ended, the Lord continued to impress on him the words from Psalm 2:8, 'Ask of me, and I will make the nations your heritage, and the ends of the earth your possession.' This passage was particularly significant because of the vast wealth C.T. was to inherit from his father, which to most men would become their heritage. By November 1884, he had requested and gotten a meeting with J. Hudson Taylor (another one of my missionary heroes), who had at that time returned to Britain to recruit more workers for his work in inland China. Studd was accepted as a missionary with Taylor's China Inland Mission and made plans to sail for Hong Kong the following February. He and some of his friends from Cambridge University decided that God was calling them to serve in China together, and as they were touring England in advance of their departure to China, they organized and led evangelistic meetings that secured support for their own work and led many toward gospel service overseas. These men, soon to be known as the Cambridge Seven, sailed for China together in February 1885.

---

1. Grubb, Norman. C.T. Studd Cricketer & Pioneer. Cambridge, England; CLC Publications

China was the first of three countries that Studd. would serve in during his missionary career. After meeting the woman who would be his wife in China, the Studds returned home to Britain, only to be called to India, where Studd planted a church and served as its pastor, until he later went to Africa as a pioneer missionary.

Studd's service in Central Africa was the most dramatic of his lifelong ministry. In 1910, after being challenged to join the work in Central Africa, he sailed for Africa alone, leaving his family behind because of the potential danger he might face. Studd had experienced some health issues during this season of his life, including severe asthma and a couple of bouts with malaria. Due to the potential residual effects of these serious illnesses, Studd was turned down both by a missionary sending agency, and because he had no money, he was also rejected by a committee of businessmen who had initially agreed to support his work in Africa. Yet Studd continued to feel strongly that God had called him to go! In his answer to the committee which had implored Studd to stay in England, he said, "Gentlemen, God has called me to go, and I will go. I will blaze the trail, though my grave may only become a stepping stone that younger men may follow."

Studd proceeded to faithfully serve the Lord in Africa for the next 21 years, with his wife serving the mission from England. His ministry in Africa saw much fruit, including many new missions stations opened and many Africans coming to know Jesus as their Lord and Savior.

Near the end of his life, Studd wrote a letter to those back home, giving a last backward look at the outstanding events of his life. The text of this letter has motivated many over the years, including myself. He wrote,

> "As I believe I am now nearing my departure from this world, I have but a few things to rejoice in; they are these: that God called me to China and I went in spite of utmost opposition from all my loved ones; that I joyfully acted as Christ told that rich young man to act; and that I deliberately at the call of God, when alone on the Bibby liner[2] in 1910, gave up my life for this work, which was to be henceforth not for the Sudan only, but for the whole unevangelized World. My only joys therefore are that when God has given me a work to do, I have not refused it."[3]

C.T. Studd fully surrendered his life to Jesus and was willing to pay any price

---

2. The name of the ship company that took him to Africa
3. Grubb, Norman. C.T. Studd Cricketer and Pioneer. Cambridge, England; CLC Publications, 1982.

for the sake of the Gospel. The story of his life is a great starting point as we look at the sixth and last of the *Marks of a Disciple of Jesus*:

Disciples of Jesus should die to themselves; that is, as a disciple pursues Jesus, they must deny themselves and take up their cross daily.

This Mark of a Disciple is the most challenging for many Christians because to fulfill this mark in your life, you much choose whom you are going to live for. There is much to lose from an earthly perspective in order to completely follow Jesus! When confronted with this choice, the decision you make demonstrates who Jesus is to you and the place in your life that He holds.

As the disciple of Jesus receives a call to follow Him, he is clearly called to deny Himself and take up his cross daily as we can read in Scripture on this topic. In three separate instances in the three different Gospel books[4], we see very similar calls by Jesus and we can also note through these examples, the true value of having different people record the events and ministry of Jesus's life. Although the three passages are very similar, we do see some slight differences, which adds to our overall understanding of the principle Jesus was teaching about. I suggest we begin this study with the passage in Luke 9 as our starting point, then we will refer to the other two passages as needed.

As we read the verses in Luke 9, we find that Jesus has sent out his twelve disciples to do ministry and they have now returned to Jesus. Upon their return, Jesus and the disciples go on a retreat to Bethsaida, for Jesus to hear the accounts of what the disciples have experienced. Jesus commences a teaching session, both to the disciples and the crowd that has followed them there.

> "And He said to all, 'If anyone would come after me, let him deny himself and take up his cross daily and follow me. For whoever would save his life will lose it, but whoever loses his life for my sake will save it. For what does it profit a man if he gains the whole world and loses or forfeits himself?'"[5]

In this teaching session, Jesus is calling all to come after Him. This phraseology is unusual to our modern English, but simply the phrase 'come after me' means anyone who would pursue Him and want to know Him better. A couple of chapters later in Luke 11, Jesus clearly sets the parameters for what this pursuit of Him should look like, as He states,

---

4. For further reading: Matthew 16:24-27, Mark 8:34-38 and Luke 9:23-25
5. Luke 9:23-25

"And I tell you, ask, and it will be given to you; seek, and you will find; knock, and it will be opened to you. For everyone who asks receives, and the one who seeks finds, and to the one who knocks it will be opened.[6]

As we look at the three action words here: *ask, seek, knock,* there is commonality among the three. All three words indicate pursuit of Jesus. We must ask, seek and knock! Jesus wants us to pursue Him actively and relentlessly, just as He actively and relentlessly pursues us. And we see His response as we pursue, 'ask, and it will be given to you; seek, and you will find; knock, and it will be opened to you.'

As we pursue Jesus and desire to be His disciples, probably the hardest part of this passage in Luke 9 for most Christians is this idea of denying ourselves, taking up our cross daily and following Jesus. I've heard more than a few Christians believe the 'cross' in this passage to mean that they have some burden that they must carry in their lives, and this is the 'cross' they must bear. To them, it may seem to mean a difficult relationship, a problem at work or a tough church situation. But I don't believe this is the meaning that Jesus was teaching here.

To a person in the first century, when a criminal carried his own cross to be crucified, the cross meant only one thing: death by the most humiliating and painful means possible. Because the Romans forced those condemned to death by crucifixion, bearing a cross meant carrying the very means that would bring about their own death, their very own execution device, while facing the jeers of ridicule on the road to their own death. It is for these reasons that this passage does not seem to be a 'I have a cross (a burden) to bear,' but rather a 'I am willing to die in order to follow Jesus' process.' And it is this "losing control of your life" aspect to these passages that many times gets whitewashed in teaching about this topic. Jesus' call here is one of complete surrender.

Remember Jesus' own words in Luke 9, "For whoever would save his life will lose it, but whoever loses his life for my sake will save it. For what does it profit a man if he gains the whole world and loses or forfeits himself?" Why is that that if you save your life, you'll lose it? That doesn't seem to make any sense! This process of losing our lives, that is, losing *control* over our lives, is what Jesus wants a disciple of His to do. He emphasizes this by saying in essence, 'You saving your life gives you no gain. The profit comes when you lose control.' When we give up our desires and our own will for our lives, that is when we truly see our best lives come to fruition!

---

6. Luke 11:9-10

Jesus isn't done with us in this passage, as He takes his teaching a step further: "For whoever is ashamed of me and of my words, of him will the Son of Man be ashamed when He comes in his glory and the glory of the Father and of the holy angels."[7] A disciple of Jesus in denying himself is also called to fully identify with Jesus. This process of 'not being ashamed' of Jesus is a big deal because it indicates total surrender and total 'buy-in.'

Jesus expounds on this thought process in Luke 18 while having a conversation with Peter: "And Peter said, 'See, we have left our homes and followed you.' And He said to them, 'Truly, I say to you, there is no one who has left house or wife or brothers or parents or children, for the sake of the kingdom of God, who will not receive many times more in this time, and in the age to come eternal life."[8] The total buy-in extends to 'no one is more important than Jesus: not friends, family, spouses… nobody.'

As we seek further understanding, the question must be asked: Why is this so hard to do? And why don't we hear more about this 'deny yourself and take up your cross' in our churches? I believe the answers to these questions are simple. First, it is a very uncomfortable message, and most churches want to attract people to attend their church services and other activities. Think about it this way: How many non-Christians would respond to a gospel presentation where the invitation was 'Come and follow Jesus, and you may face the loss of friends, family, your reputation and possibly even your life!' That wouldn't fly very well with most people and would not be very "attractional!" Instead, we rightly want to feed new inquirers of the gospel with "Gospel 101" content, just as Paul does in his first contact with the Corinthian church. In 1 Corinthians 2, he writes to them, "I fed you with milk, not solid food, for you were not ready for it. And even now you are not yet ready, for you are still of the flesh.[9]

We really need to start with this milk and not solid food as we initially present the gospel to the non-Christian. I'm afraid, though, that many of our churches get stuck in this mode and don't move their congregation any further past it. And from a fleshly perspective, I understand why they don't move any further. A Christianity where people don't have to go beyond the spiritual milk is much easier and less challenging, thereby more tempting for church leaders who want people to keep coming. I am reminded of Todd Wagner, the senior pastor at Watermark

---

7. Luke 9:26
8. Luke 18:28-30
9. 1 Corinthians 3:2-3

Community Church in Dallas and a guest whom I invited to be interviewed on my *Made for Missions*[10] podcast a couple of years ago. I love his perspective on this matter. As I mentioned in the introduction of this book, Todd said, "Most church leaders have made a deal with the people in their congregations: They say, 'You give us some money to pay some salaries and keep the lights on, and in exchange, we won't ask much of you (in terms of spiritual growth or accountability), and together we'll say we're doing everything God wants us to do.'"

But we see throughout Scripture that this is not all God wants them to do. Rather, God wants all members of the congregation to help one another grow up in Christ, to be disciples of Jesus, not just 'Sunday-only' Christians and as Paul writes to the Ephesian church, to grow "to the measure of the stature of the fullness of Christ, so that we may no longer be children, tossed to and fro by the waves and carried about by every wind of doctrine, by human cunning, by craftiness in deceitful schemes. Rather, speaking the truth in love, we are to grow up in every way into him who is the head, into Christ…"[11] Growing up in every way in Christ means taking the Six Marks of a Disciple into our churches and speaking the truth in love as we see each other's weaknesses, and helping one another grow in these six areas of our lives in Christ.

I think the second reason we struggle with denying ourselves and taking up our cross daily is that we are sinful, selfish people who, while certainly saved by grace and growing in our sanctification, will struggle with this for our whole lives, until we go home to be with the Lord. And that's why we can be horrible at this, can't we? We want to keep in control, despite all that we know in Scripture telling us that Jesus wants to 'take the wheel' of our lives. My own experience has been that, in relation to denying myself and taking up my cross daily, the biggest fight I have is with my own stubborn will that wants what I want! In my office, I have a framed graphic that is a portion of Christina Rossetti's 1876 poem *'Who shall deliver me?'* and I love to include her words in my daily prayers:

> God, harden me against myself,
>
> The coward with pathetic voice
>
> who craves for ease and rest and joy.
>
> Myself, arch-traitor to myself,

---

10. All episodes of the podcast are available on iTunes.
11. Ephesians 4:13-16

> My hollowest friend,
>
> My deadliest foe,
>
> My clog, whatever road I go.

In every way, I am always my own worst enemy when it comes to this central area of my life in Christ. I must consciously decide every day who I will live for and what steps I will take that day to live for Jesus. On at least one occasion, Jesus struggled with this Himself, as we see in His words spoken just before his own crucifixion in Luke 22, "Father, if you are willing, remove this cup from me. Nevertheless, not my will, but yours, be done."[12] This burden to take up our cross and follow Him daily is most certainly a big burden. To think the willingness necessary to endure shame, embarrassment, reproach, rejection, persecution, and even martyrdom for His sake is a lot to handle.

We must ask, then: 'How do we know if we are 'taking up our cross daily and following Jesus well' as disciples of Jesus?' You can ask yourself these questions, taken from the website www.gotquestions.org:

- Are you willing to follow Jesus if it means losing some of your closest friends?
- Are you willing to follow Jesus if it means alienation from your family?
- Are you willing to follow Jesus if it means the loss of your reputation?
- Are you willing to follow Jesus if it means losing your job?
- Are you willing to follow Jesus if it means losing your life?

Following Jesus doesn't necessarily mean all these things will happen to you, but are you *willing* to take up your cross? If there comes a point in your life where you are faced with a choice—Jesus or the comforts of this life—which will you choose?[13]

Lastly, Jesus adds a final note for those who want to be disciples of Jesus. He puts a final exclamation point on this topic in Luke 14, "Whoever does not bear his own cross and come after me cannot be my disciple. For which of you, desiring to build a tower, does not first sit down and count the cost, whether he has enough to complete it? Otherwise, when he has laid a foundation and is not able to finish,

---

12. Luke 22:42
13. "What did Jesus mean when He said, "Take up your cross and follow Me"?" Accessed October 15, 2018. https://www.gotquestions.org/take-up-your-cross.html

all who see it begin to mock him, saying, 'This man began to build and was not able to finish.'[14] In this passage, Jesus tell us we cannot be His disciple without denying ourselves and bearing his own cross. The sentences that follow are very interesting and instructive. As we continue to 'grow up in every way' in Christ, there is a counting of the costs. If we cannot or will not deny ourselves and take up our cross daily, we will be incomplete in our growing up.

Isn't C.T. Studd's life a great model for us? Studd gave up his life for the work God had called him too and acted 'joyfully' at the call of God. While I concede that God will not call all of us overseas to be missionaries as He did with C.T. Studd, his attitude of surrender to Jesus is one to be emulated, so that we too may say that the end of our lives,

> 'My only joys therefore are that when God has given me a work to do, I have not refused it.'

First Steps to Dying to Ourselves and Living for Christ

As has been now stated a few times in this book, the Six Marks of a Disciple are presented here in a particular order intentionally, because making determinations about the Marks of a Disciple in your life in the order that they are presented to you is important. As we have looked at this Mark of a Disciple, the first step is for you to determine who Jesus is to you and the value He has in your life. One way to do this is to review the notes you've made in the previous chapters and allow those notes to help you conclude if you are willing to deny yourself and take up your cross and follow Jesus. Another way is to determine what your life is worth to you and which choice (keeping control of your life or surrendering it to Jesus) is more important to you. The apostle Paul made this determination for himself and wrote about it to the Ephesian elders in Acts 20, "But I do not account my life of any value nor as precious to myself, if only I may finish my course and the ministry that I received from the Lord Jesus, to testify to the gospel of the grace of God.[15] Can you say this is true for you? If not, why not?

The second step you can take in this area is, if Paul's determination about his own life in Acts 20 does not resonate with you, identify the biggest obstacles to

---

14. Luke 14:27-30
15. Acts 20:24

seeing this Mark of a Disciple becoming true in your life. You may find a number of different obstacles and writing them down is a good first step. Invest some extended time with the Lord[16] to pray through each of these, trying to determine what needs to happen for you to find victory in each of these areas. As you pray through each point, ask Jesus to remove any spiritual strongholds that may be getting in the way of victory here. As we know, Jesus has said that the enemy, 'comes only to steal and kill and destroy. I came that they may have life and have it abundantly.'[17] Find abundant life in these areas so they are no longer points of struggle.

Finally, as you address these struggles that are keeping you from denying yourself and taking up your cross daily, and when you have spent time praying through them, make a plan to hit those obstacles head on. Here is an example of what this may look like: 'Because I allow what others think of me to dominate my life, and because I fear they would think I am crazy because I allow Jesus the #1 spot in my life, I'm going to go back to the list of Who I am in Christ in Chapter 2 of this book, and recite these truths to myself every day for a month.'

The next step to this then is to ask someone to hold you accountable to the actions you are committing to do. In this example, it may be as simple as having a friend text you one of the points from this list every day for the month, as a reminder to you. Or maybe you need to say to your accountability partner, 'If you see me failing or falling short in this area, remind me of whom I want to be and the commitments I have made in this area.' And finally, take action on the plan you have made!

Again, you may need accountability in this area. A plan is only as good as the action you take that follows!

---

16. In the Resources section of this book, I've put my notes on how to have a successful Time Alone With God, or as I call it TAWG. Adding this weekly to your schedule has many benefits!
17. John 10:10

Discussion Questions

Self-Reflection Questions

1. As you pursue Jesus, how well do you do at 'denying yourself and taking up your cross daily?'

2. What are the biggest challenges to 'denying yourself and taking up your cross daily?'

3. In the 'Are you willing…' list in this chapter, to how many of the points are you willing to commit? If there are some you are not willing to do, why are you unwilling? What would you need to do to become willing?

4. How much can you relate to Christina Rossetti's 1876 poem? What tools have you developed to 'harden yourself against yourself' to find victory in your daily walk with Jesus?

Group Discussion Questions

5. Has God called you into a work, either at home or abroad, that you need to 'deny yourself,' that is, deny your own desires and obey God in a certain work or area of your life?

6. In his final letter home to Britain, C.T. Studd had three points of joy that he felt had summarized his life. Do you have, in your own context, a similar list for your own life? If so, what are they?

7. As we read in this chapter, Paul wrote in Acts 20, "But I do not account my life of any value nor as precious to myself, if only I may finish my course and the ministry that I received from the Lord Jesus, to testify to the gospel of the grace of God." How well do you relate to his statement? If you have trouble relating, what would have to take place for you to look at your life in this way?

8. Are you prepared today to make the commitment to those in this group to pursue Jesus, deny yourselves, and take up your cross daily, knowing that we "each are the coward with pathetic voice, who craves for ease and rest and joy

Chapter 8

Living Life as a Disciple
The Six Marks of a Disciple of Jesus

The title for this book came to me in a unique way. My wife and I had a scheduled parent/teacher conference for our daughter Anna at her Middle School several years ago, to talk about her progress in an educational enhancement program in which she was enrolled. The conference was to include a learning specialist for the school district and a couple of her teachers. As we arrived for the conference, they shuttled my wife and me into a conference room at the middle school where the meeting was to be held. As we sat down at the conference table, I looked to my left and saw a poster taped on the wall of the conference room. In bright primary colors, the poster instantly caught my eye with these words, 'What you do shows who you are.' In the same category with posters that I bet you have seen in many classrooms (if you've been in an American classroom in the past ten years!), this one was much like the ever popular 'Attitudes are contagious…is yours worth catching?' or the omnipresent 'Today is a great day to learn something new!' When I read this poster, I instantly reminded myself of how true the saying was, and in the intervening weeks and months, I couldn't get the phrase out of my head! The more I thought about it, the more I saw the wisdom in it because yes, it is quite true. What you do really does show who you are. If you are a nice person, you'll say and do nice things. And if you are a mean person, you will say and do things that are mean or hurtful to others. So, if you want to know what type of person someone is, watch what they do and how they act!

The Six Marks of a Disciple of Jesus that I have outlined here are markers in your pursuit of being a disciple of Jesus. While we know that God is in charge of our spiritual growth, if you see these marks in your life, you are a disciple--and if you don't see these marks with much regularity, may this book be an encouragement to you to take a look at areas that need growth in your walk with Jesus.

As we are finishing our study of the Six Marks of a Disciple of Jesus, I believe that if you've made it to this point in this book, you do want to be a disciple of Jesus. I also know that not one of us wants to be thought of or seen as a 'Sunday-only' Christian, one who shows up at church on Sundays but does not think about Jesus again until the next Sunday. As you've read through this book, you have hopefully been challenged and have seen some areas that you are working on and growing in as you desire to be a disciple of Jesus.

A statement that I think we all can agree on: working on becoming a disciple of Jesus is hard work, isn't it? And it most definitely is something we'll be working on for our whole lives, as Jesus desires us to renounce all for Him. Please don't be fooled: this renouncing all is gut-wrenching, soul-crushing work at times as we struggle as humans to get out of our own way to allow Jesus to do the work He wants to do in us.

In bringing this study 'home,' I'd like to draw out three final points as we finish this study together: First, a few principles about being a disciple of Jesus that will wrap this study up nicely can be found in Luke 14, so let's look at the passage from this chapter of Luke together. Secondly, I think it's appropriate to look at what being a disciple of Jesus looks like from day-to-day, so I'll give you a few ideas that have worked for me and that, hopefully, will be helpful to you as well. Finally, I'll end this chapter with some final steps we can all take as we desire to be a disciple of Jesus.

As you probably recall from the last chapter, I mentioned the very challenging passage in Luke 14 that I think defines the essence of what it means to be a disciple of Jesus. Read this passage again, and allow it to sink in. You may want to read it through a few times and allow your mind and your heart to marinate on this passage.

> "Now great crowds accompanied him, and He turned and said to them, "If anyone comes to me and does not hate his own father and mother and wife and children and brothers and sisters, yes, and even his own life, he **cannot be my disciple**. Whoever does not bear his own cross and come after me **cannot be my disciple**. For which of you, desiring to build a tower, does not first sit down and count the cost, whether he has enough to complete it? Otherwise, when he has laid a foundation and is not able to finish, all who see it begin to mock him, saying, 'This man began to build and was not able to finish.' Or what king, going out to encounter another king in war, will not sit down first and deliberate whether he is able with ten thousand to meet him who comes against him with twenty thousand? And if not, while the other is yet a great way off, he sends a delegation and asks for terms of peace. So therefore, any one of you who does not renounce all that he has **cannot be my disciple**."[1]

We need to examine four sections of this passage in order to fully understand it. In the first part, Jesus gives us a big challenge about our own familial relationships—that we must hate them, or we cannot be his disciple. These are definitely harsh words, especially when we give such high priority to the value of marriage and family relationships in our churches today. Perhaps we can soften the sharpness of these words of Jesus a bit by remembering that the Hebrew mind of Jesus' day moved in contrasts and extremes; darkness and light, falsehood and truth, love and hate – often with no shades of gray. Jesus Himself dearly loved His own mother and even as He was dying on the cross, He wanted to ensure that she would be cared for after His departure.[2] Jesus' admonition to hate our family was not, I think an actual call to *hate* them, but rather a call that a disciple of His must put Jesus in the *very first place* among all our relational loyalties. In that light, we must note what comes after this call to hate family for His sake: If you don't, you can't be His disciple.

The second part of this passage is one I dove into deeply in Chapter 7, that 'Whoever does not bear his own cross and come after me cannot be my disciple.' While I would encourage you to re-read that section of Chapter 7, I have often noted in this passage how many times Jesus says, 'if you do this or don't do that, you cannot be my disciple.' In fact, I have highlighted in bold the instances He

---

1. Luke 14:25-33
2. John 19:25-27

says this explicitly: three times in nine verses! I have always found Jesus' choice of words to be interesting when He says 'cannot.' Jesus doesn't say that if you don't love Him above all else, *He* won't allow you to be His disciple. The Greek word here is *Dynatai*, which suggests 'not possible.' In other words, it is *not possible* to be Jesus' disciple without doing these things! A failure to commit yourself to Jesus exclusively and unconditionally is not compatible with what it means to be a follower of Jesus Christ.

Jesus then says 'For which of you, desiring to build a tower, does not first sit down and count the cost, whether he has enough to complete it? Otherwise, when he has laid a foundation and is not able to finish, all who see it begin to mock him, saying, 'This man began to build and was not able to finish.' Or what king, going out to encounter another king in war, will not sit down first and deliberate whether he is able with ten thousand to meet him who comes against him with twenty thousand? And if not, while the other is yet a great way off, he sends a delegation and asks for terms of peace.' This passage may require a second look in order to understand it in the context of the rest of the passage, but the meaning soon becomes clear: just in the same way that you don't begin building a house without knowing you have what it takes to finish, our relationship with Jesus is the same: you should not get into it unless you can fully commit to Him! This is one of the unique mysteries about accepting Christ: the salvation that He offers is both free and it also costs you your very life! It costs you nothing but once you receive it, you have just committed everything you are and have to Jesus. Many may protest that as a contradiction: how can something be both free and cost everything at the same time?

I often explain this by using the example of marriage, as the requirements Jesus sets before us sound to me a lot like what is expected in a lasting marriage. It seems to me that the commitments made in a marriage are just as exclusive, just as demanding and unconditional as what Jesus sets before us. In most wedding ceremonies, the pastor will say something along these lines to the groom, 'Will you have this woman to be your wedded wife? Will you love her, comfort her, honor and keep her for better or worse, for richer and poorer, in sickness and in health, to love and to cherish and, forsaking all others, keep yourself only unto her, so long as you both shall live?' The pastor then asks the same questions to the bride. What these two people are really asking each other is "Will you make me the preeminent person in your life? Will you set aside your parents, your sisters and brothers, and all your other acquaintances and friends and devote yourself first and foremost to me?" All of these requests are incredibly demanding, and yet these two people are counting the costs of what type of commitments they are prepared to make to enter into this relationship – "no other lovers on the side, no secret bank accounts and no one else on this earth gets more of my time than you." I always marvel that this commitment…. it's serious! And yet, even as the two people join together in marriage, they do so willingly, and yes, even delight in the opportunity to get married and make these commitments. They are not thinking about what they have to give up, only what they are gaining! Becoming a disciple of Jesus is like that as well. A disciple is one who wants to gain Christ. As we saw in Chapter 2, as we consider the attributes of Christ and the transformation from death to life that has occurred in our lives, the disciple of Jesus goes with joy to give up everything else for Jesus. He's worth the sacrifice!

As it relates to marriage, a disturbing trend is growing in our culture these days. More and more couples are not making the traditional marriage commitment but are rather simply living together. I recently saw a study online that 40% of children in the United States are now born out of wedlock.[3] On one hand from a worldly perspective, it may seem like cohabiting together makes sense. After all, who buys a car without test driving it first? Living together first before making a big commitment would make sense, right? And by cohabiting, it allows the two people to keep options open and after all, if they love each other, that's all that counts. Of course, the problem is that this arrangement isn't a trial marriage at all, because it lacks the one thing that defines a marriage: an exclusive, committed lifelong relationship! People who simply cohabitate together are deceived into thinking they are experiencing marriage. They are not—and are settling for a poor imitation of the commitment that can only come when they commit to one another fully with their hearts and souls in an exclusive love that only death can destroy. I fear that far too many Christians today are settling for this 'half-in, half-out, I'll stay engaged as long as it benefits me' attitude toward Jesus.

Jesus puts an exclamation point on His teaching in Luke 14 as He states that He wants undeniably the number one spot in your life. He wants all of you and is saying that to be his disciple, you must put Jesus in first place among all your

---

3. https://ifstudies.org/blog/how-we-ended-up-with-40-percent-of-children-born-out-of-wedlock

relational loyalties. Any one of you who is not fully devoted to me, He says, anyone who does not give up his claim of ownership on everything he has and even his own life cannot be my disciple. He states, "So therefore, any one of you who does not renounce all that he has cannot be my disciple." Do you want to be a disciple of Jesus? Giving Him the first spot in your life is the goal of your life from today until forever. The apostle Paul gives us such a great picture of what this looks like in his life. In Philippians 3, Paul is warning the Philippian church of 'evildoers,' who put their confidence in the flesh. Paul states that he has more reason to boast in the flesh and in his status in life than most anyone else. But he rejects that lifestyle and states that "whatever gain I had, I counted as loss for the sake of Christ. Indeed, I count everything as loss because of the surpassing worth of knowing Christ Jesus my Lord. For his sake I have suffered the loss of all things and count them as rubbish, in order that I may gain Christ and be found in him, not having a righteousness of my own that comes from the law, but that which comes through faith in Christ."[4] For the disciple of Jesus, our daily discipline becomes one of casting off the temporary gains of this world in favor of the eternal worth of knowing Jesus better and more intimately every day.

So, what does this look like day-to-day? Let's assume I'm convincing you that Jesus really does want it all…. What happens now? There are three quick thoughts that you can implement into your own life that may be helpful for you as well:

1. We must continuously work on doing the things that Jesus specifically says to do. In Luke 6, Jesus pointedly asks us "Why do you call me 'Lord, Lord,' and not do what I tell you?"[5] I wish that in our churches today this passage was emphasized more since we certainly are calling Him 'Lord,' but don't talk much about what He's telling us to do. For the disciple of Jesus, His direct instructions are my treasures for living life. We will work and train ourselves to both know and obey what Jesus says to do. This leads to our inward transformation by grace to become the person God wants us to be.

2. As we conduct the everyday activities of life, at home, at school, in our community, in our career, we do so in the character and power of Christ. Having surrendered our lives to Him, He will show us how to live. His character, power and personal guidance will lead us into life as it should be in all areas of human existence!

---

4. Philippians 3:7-9a
5. Luke 6:46

3. Finally, we continually orient our values to reflect Jesus, who is holding the greatest value in our lives. Being His disciple is an orientation and quality of our entire existence. We may not choose anything to be of greater value than Jesus and His Kingdom. Once this orientation is in place, the Holy Spirit can begin to move throughout every aspect of what we are and what we do. But we are not passive in this process. As Paul writes in Colossians, "seeing that you have put off the old self with its practices and have put on the new self, which is being renewed in knowledge after the image of its creator." [6]

If you feel overwhelmed and exhausted just by reading this chapter, you are not alone! But it is clear that Jesus wants all our lives as His disciples, not just part of us. Over the course of my life with Christ, I've found that puttin Him in the driver's seat of my life is a daily decision. I fail often, and I curse this imperfect shell of flesh that I am in, and I ask Jesus for help to defeat my selfish desires. And all the while, I am especially thankful that even as I fall off the 'horse,' I dust myself off and repeat to myself 1 John 1:9, "If we confess our sins, He is faithful and just to forgive us our sins and to cleanse us from all unrighteousness." I often say to Jesus, "Lord, I know that I fall short of your best for my life. I confess that 'x, y and z' happened and I'm thankful that you have forgiven me already. I want to deny myself and be your disciple today. Please reveal to me what areas I need to surrender to you today to make that happen."

The Struggle is Real

In writing this book, I asked ten friends to proofread the book for me before I called the manuscript finished. I felt it was an important step to ask people I trusted a few questions like, 'How does this book hit you? How does it read? In your opinion, is it theologically accurate?' While I received a lot of good feedback, it was the feedback from Lisa, a friend of my wife and me, that hit me the hardest. Lisa shared with me about a time in her life that she felt completely overwhelmed as a young mom and wife. Observing other Christians who didn't seem to be struggling in their relationship with God in the same way that she did, it all got to be too hard for her. She began to retreat in her relationship with God, believing that this vibrant

---

6. Colossians 3:9-10

relationship with God that would lead to victory in the Six Marks of a Disciple that I mention in this book were attainable only by 'Super Christians.' Then came a day that served as a turning point in her relationship with God. Unsure of where to turn her relationship around with God, she simply committed to spend the first part of every day with God, in prayer and in His Word. In her own words, "That day marked a turning point in my life that completely transformed my walk of faith. The enemy had blinded me[7], but God opened my eyes afresh to what having a personal relationship with him was and is really like and the Bible came alive for me in ways it never had before. I could not get enough of it and the transforming work God had been wanting to do in me finally began to take root and bear fruit." Lisa's story is such a good testimony of what God wants to do in our lives as we trust Him. As we end our Six Marks journey together, if you will put your complete trust in Him and 'renounce all,' amazing things can happen!

So if you have read this book and you are at a life stage like Lisa's where you are struggling to believe that God can help you find victory in the Six Marks I have outlined through Scripture, may I encourage you in a few specific areas today?

First, if you have been reading about these Six Marks and thinking, 'These are for Super Christians only and there's no way I could ever see victory in these areas,' I would encourage you to tell God what you are thinking and admit to Him the areas where you struggle. Be honest with God! It certainly won't hurt given that He already knows all that you are thinking anyway. Is there a roadblock that you can't seem to figure out? Give it to God and allow Him to be the one to remove it.

Maybe these Six Marks cause you to feel angry or upset. Tell that to God, because our emotions matter to Him! We already know from previous chapters of this book that God loves you regardless of where you struggle or what you are feeling. Remember what we studied in Chapter 2 about what God thinks of us and how our identify in Christ has been changed forever. So, if He loves you endlessly, why not be totally honest with God about what your struggle is and why you think you cannot find victory? He's the One who is in control of your growth. Our job is to 'renounce all,' tell Him we want to become more like Jesus and allow Him to do the work in our lives that He wants to do.

---

7. John 10:10

The Role of the Local Church in Helping People Become Disciples of Jesus

I would be remiss if, in this chapter on *Living Life as a Disciple of Jesus*, I did not mention the role of the local church in helping you become a disciple of Jesus. I have written about six particular marks you'll find in a disciple of Jesus, and much of this book is an individual look at your life and how you can grow in these six areas in your relationship with Jesus. But I cannot overstate the importance of the accountability and community that is found in a body of believers who want to help each other grow as disciples of Jesus. The process of how the local church can help their people become committed disciples of Jesus is a multi-layered one It begins with elders (biblical word for the leaders of a church) who view their role from a biblical perspective.

One of the favorite verses that boards of elders like to quote to their congregation is Hebrews 13:17, "Obey your leaders and submit to them, for they are keeping watch over your souls, as those who will have to give an account. Let them do this with joy and not with groaning, for that would be of no advantage to you." While this is an instructive verse for the congregation of a biblical mandate to obey their leaders, I often focus on the second part of the verse, the responsibility of elders as the congregation submits to their God-given authority. Elders are called by God to keep watch over souls, as those who will have to give an account. This 'account,' is literally a speech that will have to be given before God in heaven on how they did at keeping watch over those put in their charge. If I were a church elder, I would want to ensure that I had a good answer for how I did at the job God gave me to do. I often encourage church leaders to major in a couple of areas in their churches so as to make sure that speech is followed by a 'well done, good and faithful servant.'[8]

A High Value on the Word of God

A couple of times in this book, I have mentioned Todd Wagner, Pastor of Watermark Community Church in Dallas, Texas. In my journey toward learning about these Six Marks, about Great Commission fulfillment, and about how a church can do this well, Todd has provided an invaluable example. If you talk to the staff at Watermark about what it's like to work on staff, you will hear a couple of

---

8. Matthew 25:23

dominant principles from almost every staff member. The first thing you'll hear is how important it is to Todd and the other leaders to do biblical conflict resolution well. They work really hard on resolving conflicts well. The second thing you will hear is that Todd, almost every time you see him in-person, will ask you "So what are you learning from God's Word lately?"

I love this question and its frequency for several reasons: first, it places a high value on spending time in God's Word. It's almost as if Todd is saying, "Of all the topics you and I could talk about (the local sports team, the weather, your job, etc.), the most important is that you are investing time in God Word. It's what we do around here." The second thing I love about this is that if the Senior Pastor is going to be asking you what you're learning from God's Word every time you see him, you want to have a good answer! In other words, you'd better be spending time in God's Word! The leadership team of a church can help its people grow in the Marks of a Disciple by stressing—and yes, even expecting its congregation to be spending time daily in God's word.

Biblical Community or Small Group Emphasis

Spiritual growth happens largely within a biblical community of believers who also want to grow spiritually. Biblical community connects people in authentic relationships that lead to spiritual transformation. While there are several ministries that a church can provide to help its congregation grow spiritually, doing biblical community well is at the top of my list! I have heard countless testimonies of how God has used biblical community to radically change people's lives, transforming them to be more like Jesus. You will want to pursue community not only to make new Christian friends with whom you can study the Bible, but I believe that there is something even greater that happens within biblical community. I encourage you to pray that God will use biblical community to make you more like Jesus![9] While that is a big target to aim toward, walking through life with other believers who also want to be disciples of Jesus is the path toward spiritual growth. As we read in Ecclesiastes 4, "Two are better than one, because they have a good reward for their toil. For if they fall, one will lift up his fellow. But woe to him who is alone when he falls and has not another to lift him up!"[10]

---

9. Romans 8:29
10. Ecclesiastes 4:9-10

Continual Training and Study Opportunities

As I've previously mentioned, I believe the very first thing that church leaders should be doing in the area of training is to teach their people how to share the Gospel and give a simple testimony. In addition to this, having regular classes throughout the year, equipping their congregation to take continual steps toward a more intimate, closer relationship with God by learning and practicing the basics of the Christian faith is so important. Areas of training like the basic disciplines of the Christian walk to training on God's Word, prayer and fellowship allow the elder to answer the Hebrews 13:17 question and ensure that his people are growing toward victory in the Six Marks of a Disciple.

Final Steps toward Being a Disciple of Jesus

Becoming a disciple of Jesus is a daily pursuit of casting off the world for the surpassing worth of knowing Jesus more intimately. Here are three steps that we all can be working on toward that goal. The first step in this direction involves developing a spiritual discipline in the area of choosing Christ over all else. I call this a discipline because it does take time to develop the conviction that, if we have to choose between Christ and anything else, we choose Christ. Some may call it a 'second sense' in honoring the place that Christ holds in our lives. This come in handy so much in my own life. While it's easier to give in or to not want to 'make a scene,' honoring that place that Jesus demands in our lives is so important. In many situations, God may not bring us to this point, but as we need to do so, we have already resolved in our hearts that as the choice needs to be made, we choose Christ.

Secondly, we follow Paul's lead in dealing with all of life's situations in a way that draw us nearer to Christ. Remembering his admonition that 'for his sake I have suffered the loss of all things and count them as rubbish, in order that I may gain Christ and be found in him,' we work on gaining that perspective in every situation that we run across in our lives. We can hold on to everything pleasant by being thankful for Christ, and we will endure the hurtful situations by being patient through Christ.

Thirdly, we begin to see the world differently through the lens of "counting all as lost for Christ." I often think of the common phrase that comes up when talking about one's death that 'You never see a moving van following a hearse.' This step conditions our heart to see things of this world that, although useful, carry no eternal value. If we lose any of the material things that this world has to offer, we don't lose our joy because the things of this world are not our treasure.

Final Words

I hope this book has been helpful in your spiritual growth as you pursue the process of becoming a disciple of Jesus. Each of the Marks we've studied can be reviewed many times over in your spiritual growth pursuit, and as I wrote earlier in this book, this journey is done best with others. I hope and pray that you've been able to go through this book with a community of like-minded believers who want to be disciples of Jesus also and know that accountability is a key part of this process, and that you may then choose to use this book to walk with new believers as they learn about growing in their faith. I hope and pray that this book launches you into a lifetime pursuit of Jesus!

Discussion Questions

Self-Reflection Questions

1. We need to do the actions that Jesus specifically tells us to do as a Disciple of Jesus. How have you grown in this area since reading Chapter 4 on being obedient to the Bible? What are the parallels you've drawn between the two principles?

2. In Philippians 3, Paul writes that "whatever gain I had, I counted as loss for the sake of Christ. Indeed, I count everything as loss because of the surpassing worth of knowing Christ Jesus my Lord." In what ways does that motivate you, and in what ways might it make you twinge as you think of your life?

3. As most of us are living in economic areas that are considered 'First World,' what are the biggest temptations that get in our way of 'counting all as loss' for Jesus?

4. How are you currently dealing with all of life's situations in ways that draw you nearer to Christ? In what areas do you need help or encouragement?

Group Discussion Questions

5. In Luke 14, Jesus states on three occasions that we 'cannot' be His disciple without doing the actions outlined. Does this strong statement of 'cannot' motivate you toward moving the *'cannot'* to *'can'* in these three areas of your life?

6. As stated in this chapter, 'Being His disciple is an orientation and quality of my entire existence. There must be nothing held of greater value than Jesus and His Kingdom.' In what areas of your life could you orient better toward Jesus being held of greatest value?

7. As it relates to developing a discipline in the area of choosing Christ over all else, in what ways are you already doing that? In what areas of your life do you need to work?

8. As you've got through this book with a small group or Sunday School class, in what ways can you continue encouraging one another to be disciples of Jesus daily?

Resources

As an addition to this book, I have included a number of tools that I've found useful over the years in my own walk with Jesus. One of favorite verses of all time in the Bible is from 2 Timothy, "Do your best to present yourself to God as one approved, a worker who has no need to be ashamed, rightly handling the word of truth."[1] Paul's admonition to Timothy is a good one for us today because it indicates action, that there are things to be done if we do not want to be ashamed. The biggest action here is to rightly handle the word of truth. But what how do we rightly handle the word of truth? I think we do this by studying it, talking about it with others and preparing for opportunities to share it with others. It's my hope that the tools included in the Resources section will lead you to a life of presenting yourself to God as a person who takes His Word seriously in your life and can correctly handle it.

For each tool, I'm including a brief introduction of what the particular tool is, how to use it and why I deemed it important to include here in the Appendix. Each of the tools are also available at www.SixMarks.org, where you'll find a printable version that you can use for handouts, either for your own personal use, or to share with others who are going through this book as a group. I hope that each of these tools is a blessing and a benefit to you all!

---

1. 2 Timothy 2:15

Extended Time Alone with God (TAWG)

Almost every Friday that I'm in town, usually from 9AM until about noon, I invest some extended time with God at my favorite outdoor location near my house. I've been purposefully setting aside this time for years. and I find it to be a very valuable investment of my time. For many, the idea of this much extended time in prayer can seem so difficult that they never get to it! But this extended time with the Lord is one of the best investments of your time that you can ever make!

This Time Alone with God, or as I like to call it, TAWG, is in addition to your Quiet Times that you spend daily with the Lord. The biggest benefit that I find in these extended periods of time is that it really gives you additional time to praise God and to then hear from Him. I often tell people that I need the first hour to just clear my head of all the distractions: stuff going on at home, on my job, in my marriage, with my kids, etc. Once my mind is cleared, I still have an hour or two to really commune with the Lord and begin to hear clear direction from Him. Here are some highlights of how you can begin adding a TAWG to your schedule, and some step-by-step directions on how to make it work.

Finding a Place to Go

Finding an outdoor setting has worked incredibly well for me, so if you can, I highly recommend that you find an outdoor location for your extended time with the Lord. (Here in Colorado, sometimes an outdoor location doesn't work well, especially in the winter. In those times, I huddle in my basement office!)

Here are a couple of keys for your search: Finding a place where you can be as uninterrupted as possible is a good rule of thumb. Also, there's just something 'magic' about being outside! In the place where I like to go, I can see the Front Range of the Rocky Mountains just west of Denver, and as I am praying and reading Scripture, I can sense and feel God in powerful ways. I often say to the Lord as I'm looking out at the mountains, 'Lord, if you created all of this, and I know You did, anything I bring to You, I am confident You can handle!'

How to Invest your Time

This extended time with God is a great opportunity to connect with God and hear from Him. Let's assume that you decide to dedicate three hours to this time with God, as I often do. You can divide your time between reading Scripture, meditating on the Scripture you read, praying to God and dedicating some time to just being silent before God to hear from Him. While you certainly don't have to do this in just the same way that I do, a good first step would be to split the time into thirds. For the first third of the time, read and pray through Scripture of your choosing. For the second third, invest time praying to the Lord, and for the final third, dedicate that remaining time to hear from God, being silent before the Lord and hearing from Him.

If you may have never 'heard' from God or know how that may occur, please allow me to try to describe briefly how that normally happens. While God can speak to us in a myriad of ways, such as through angels, visions or miraculous events, you will generally find that God will speak to you through your thoughts. He will use times when you are reading the Bible, praying quietly, or seeking counsel from other Christians as you talk to them about a situation you're trying to figure out.

Here is an example of "hearing from God" that happened in my own life recently. A couple of years ago, I was sensing that perhaps God was asking me to lead our ministry in a different direction. We were doing Bible distribution events in China and I loved the work. As we began to have difficulty finding places to go to distribute Bibles to Christians in rural China where Bibles are not readily accessible, I began asking the Lord what His will was for next steps. As I invested extended time with Him, a deep heart for the people groups around the world that had never heard about Jesus began to well up in my mind. I began to see the passages of Scripture that talk about God's plan for the nations in a new way, and I heard God's 'still, small voice' in my head. I also began to 'run into' people who were doing this work and after hearing of the over 4,000 people groups not yet reached for the Gospel from them, I knew God was leading us to contribute to this need.

After you have some experience doing this exercise, you will find the rhythm and flow that works best for you.

What to take with you

There are a few 'must have' items that you will want to have with you: Bible, paper, and a pen or pencil. Other helpful items might include:

- A favorite devotional book
- Your current prayer list
- Your quiet time journal (or an empty journal for you to begin one!)
- Scripture memory cards
- Notes from your last extended time in prayer

How to stay awake and alert

- Get adequate rest the night before.
- Change positions—sit a while, walk around, sit, walk, and repeat.
- Create variety in what you do. Read the Scriptures, then pray, then write, and so on.
- Pray aloud—in a whisper or soft voice if necessary. For those who love to worship God with music, having a playlist of worship songs on your smartphone may help keep you focused!

Taking notes

Taking notes during your extended time with God will give you a record of the thoughts and words the Lord is speaking to you, as well as helping you keep your time organized.

In addition, when we pray, we often have something come to mind that we feel we should take action on, or that we have forgotten to do—perhaps totally unrelated to what we are praying about. By keeping paper or your device ready to list these things, we can avoid prolonged distraction and then act on them later.

Toward the end of your time in prayer, you will want to spend a few minutes writing down some conclusions. Summarize the major impressions of your time. Keep these notes in a notebook and review them weekly for a while. This will ensure that you follow through on the concepts, commands, or ideas that God has impressed upon you.

A Couple of Closing Thoughts

Lorne Sanny was discipled by The Navigators' founder Dawson Trotman and served as The Navigators General Director for thirty years. I close this resource with a couple of encouraging quotes from him on spending extended time with God.

"The result of your day in prayer should be answers to the two questions Paul asked the Lord on the Damascus road (Acts 22:6-10). Paul's first question was, 'Who are you, Lord?' The Lord replied, 'I am Jesus.' You will be seeking to know Him, to find out who He is. The second question Paul asked was, 'What shall I do, Lord?' and the Lord answered him specifically. This should be answered or reconfirmed for you in that part of the day when you unhurriedly seek His will for you."

"Don't think you must end the day with some new discovery or extraordinary experience. Wait on God and expose yourself to His Word. Looking for a new experience or insight you can share with someone when you get back will get you off the track. True, you may gain some new insight, but often this can just take your attention from the real business. The test of such a day is not how exhilarated we are when the day is over but how it works into life tomorrow. If we have really exposed ourselves to the Word and come into contact with God, it will affect our daily life. God bless you as you do this—and do it soon!"[1]

---

1. https://www.navigators.org/resource/spend-extended-time-prayer/

Sharing Your Testimony

As already stated in this book, I think the disciple of Jesus must be always "prepared to make a defense to anyone who asks you for a reason for the hope that is in you." As you prepare your testimony, this outline has been found useful by many for writing down the story of how you came to know Jesus as your Lord and Savior. As you answer the questions on this page, you can then use your answers to form a 3-6 minute testimony of God's goodness in your life. A printable version of this worksheet can be found at SixMarks.org and can be freely used as a handout.

After answering the questions, remember to practice it a lot! In this case, practice really does make perfect! Practice it so many times that you can easily repeat it to someone who asks you about how to became a Christian.

Pre-flight

Colossians 4:5-6

I Peter 3:15

Before I Accepted Christ (or gave Him complete control)

1. What was my life like that will relate most to the non-Christian?

2. What did my life revolve around the most? Where did I find my security or happiness? (The non-Christian is relying on something external to give him happiness)

3. How did those areas begin to let me down?

How I Received Christ (or gave Him complete control)

1. When was the first time I heard the gospel? (Or when was I exposed to dynamic Christianity)

2. What were my initial reactions?

3. When did my attitude begin to turn around? Why?

4. What were the final struggles that went through my mind just before I accepted Christ?

5. Why did I go ahead and accept Christ?

After I Accepted Christ (or gave Him complete control)

1. Specific changes and illustrations about the changes Christ has made:

2. Why am I motivated differently?

Helpful Hints

1. Write the way you speak; making the testimony yours.

2. Practice this over and over until it becomes natural.

3. Shoot for short: 3-6 minutes. At that length, it's easily something you can put into a conversation without it becoming a monologue.

Three-Point Topical Bible Study

I have used this simple Bible study tool a lot over the years. Feel free to make copies of the version you find on www.SixMarks.org, and use it as you study God's Word. I think you'll find the steps for using it to be pretty self-explanatory.

Topic or Heading_____

Verses_____

1. What are some main facts and statements in this passage?

2. How would I explain some words and statements in this passage to make them clearer? (or what words or phrases would I like to have explained?)

3. What is most helpful to me in this passage?

Spiritual Gifts Study

The subject of spiritual gifts is often misunderstood. What are spiritual gifts, and how does God use them within His Church? They are abilities given to individual Christians by the Holy Spirit that enable them to participate in His work and His mission on earth. Each person who has trusted Christ as their Lord and Savior has at least one spiritual gift, and we read in Hebrews 2 that the 'gifts of the Holy Spirit are distributed according to his will.'[1] (Through experience and testing, I believe I have at least three: Faith, Discerning Between Spirits and Apostleship.)

Spiritual gifts are different from natural talents in that a natural talent is a physical ability to do some activities better than others, like musical ability, mechanical aptitude or artistic skills. God can use these too, but a spiritual gift is a spiritual ability. Interestingly, natural talents are often the mode by which spiritual gifts can be used. For example, someone with a mechanical aptitude may have the spiritual gift of evangelism and while helping someone with a car repair, he or she may very naturally use that opportunity to have a spiritual conversation with the person who is being helped.

There are three main passages of Scripture that lay out for us the spiritual gifts that God gives to us as we accept Christ. Hopefully this resource will help you to discover what your spiritual gifts may be.

Below you will find each spiritual gift located under the heading of each of the passages where it is found, so that if you would want to read about them in the Bible, you'll know where they are found.

1 Corinthians 12:8

Wisdom - to apply knowledge to life in such a way as to make spiritual truths quite relevant and practical in proper decision-making and daily life situations[2].

Knowledge - to seek to learn as much about the Bible as possible through the gathering of much information and the analysis of that data.

1 Corinthians 12:9

Faith - to be firmly persuaded of God's power and promises to accomplish His will and purpose and to display such a confidence in Him and His Word that

---

1. Hebrews 2:4
2. Definitions for each spiritual gift loosely taken from the website https://mintools.com/gifts-list.htm

circumstances and obstacles do not shake that conviction.

Healing - to be used as a means through which God makes people whole either physically, emotionally, mentally, or spiritually.

1 Corinthians 12:10

Miraculous Powers – This spiritual gift is different than healing, in that those with this gift can bring about supernatural events that occur outside the bounds of what is natural. Casting out of demons[3] and raising people from the dead[4] may be a couple of biblical examples. (And before you cast this gift aside as inactive in modern times, I have heard of multiple stories of these types of events continuing to happen in our ministry in China).

Prophecy - to speak forth the message of God to His people.

Distinguishing Between Spirits (sometimes referred to as **Discernment**) - to clearly distinguish truth from error by judging whether the behavior or teaching is from God, Satan, human error, or human power.

Speaking in tongues - to speak in a language not previously learned through one's own human efforts, for the purpose of allowing unbelievers to hear God's message in their own language or the Church to be edified.

1 Corinthians 12:28

Helps - to render support or assistance to others in the body so as to free them for ministry to others. Those with this gift often seem to know just the right thing to do to be of greatest assistance.

Administration - to steer the body toward the accomplishment of God-given goals and directives by planning, organizing, and supervising others.

1 Corinthians 14

Speaking in Tongues - See note above from I Corinthians 12. For this to be a biblical spiritual gift, someone must be present who is able to interpret the language.

1 Corinthians 14:7

Service - to identify undone tasks in God's work, however menial, and use available resources to get the jobs done.

---

3. Acts 16
4. Acts 9

Teaching - to instruct others in the Bible in a logical, systematic way so as to communicate pertinent information for true understanding and growth.

1 Corinthians 14:8

Encouraging (sometimes referred to as Exhortation) – to sense someone's need for encouragement and then come alongside someone with words of comfort, consolation, and counsel to help them be all God wants them to be.

Contributing to the needs of others - to willingly share one's material resources with liberality and cheerfulness, and without thought of being repaid.

Leadership - to stand before people in such a way as to attend to the direction of the church body with such care and diligence so as to motivate others to get involved in the accomplishment of these goals.

Mercy – spiritual sensitivity toward those who are suffering, whether physically, mentally, or emotionally, so as to feel genuine sympathy with their misery, speaking words of compassion and caring for them with deeds of love to help alleviate their distress.

Ephesians 4:11

Apostleship[5] (sometimes referred to as Missionary, although I'm not personally a fan of that designation) – to plant new ministries and churches, go into places where the Gospel is not preached, reach across cultures to establish churches in challenging environments, raise up and develop leaders, call out and lead pastors and shepherds, and much more.

Prophecy - to speak forth the message of God to His people.

Evangelism - to be a gifted messenger of the good news of the Gospel.

Pastor - to be responsible for spiritually caring for, protecting, guiding, and teaching a group of believers entrusted to one's care.

Teacher - to instruct others in the Bible in a logical, systematic way so as to communicate pertinent information for true understanding and growth.

---

5. The spiritual gift of apostleship is sometimes confused with the office of Apostle. The office of Apostle was held by a limited number of men chosen by Jesus including the twelve disciples (Mark 3:13-19) and Paul (Romans 1:1). The office of Apostle was a one-time office for those who were doing ministry with Jesus and the apostle Paul. The spiritual gift of apostleship is an active spiritual gift that the Holy Spirit gives to people today!

Sharing the Gospel through the Bridge Illustration

While there are many ways to share the Gospel, and many ways that are effective, I have found the bridge illustration to be one of the very best methods.

Why do I think it's the very best? Several reasons: first, you can write it out on anything. I've drawn out the bridge illustration on a napkin in a restaurant, on a pizza box in the dorm, and in one case, on a man's arm! You can write it out anywhere! Secondly, you only need to memorize six verses in order to give a clear presentation of the Gospel. While I have a version of the bridge for you here, please go to www.SixMarks.org to print our official version, and if you go to the *One Eight Catalyst* You Tube channel, you can view a 15-minute video of me teaching you how to share the Gospel through the bridge illustration.

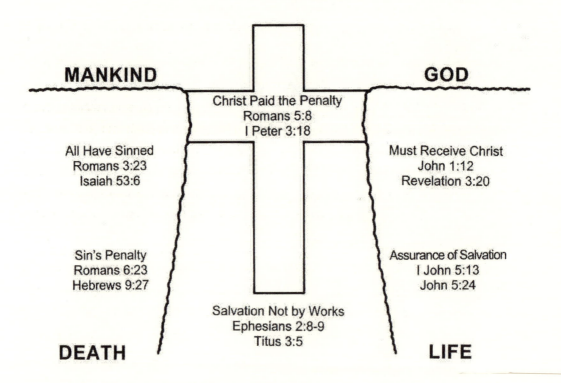

Leader's Guide

What You Do Shows Who You Are

If you are leading a group of people through this book, this Leader's Guide is designed for you!

This leader's guide is designed for those of you who are leading your class or small group through this book. My hope in providing a Leader's Guide is to help you teach your people this content and for them to get the most benefit from it. As you will see as you read through the book, this is very challenging material that will stretch all those who read it and take it to heart. I hope that you will be able to see a transformation in the individuals participating in your class or small group as they find areas where growth can be had in their own lives and in their walk with Jesus.

Naturally, it will be vitally important that you will have read the chapter and gone through the 8 Discussion questions yourself before you teach. If you have one hour of teaching time per chapter, I recommend that you teach on that chapter for about 20 minutes, then allow 30 minutes for discussion in the group or class and invest the last 10 minutes in developing Action Steps for each person to follow through. In this leader's guide, I'm giving you additional material you can use to teach your small group or class.

This leader's guide includes several sections. Here is a quick rundown of each section and its purpose:

Opening Paragraph

Initially, I will provide some additional insight into the chapter for you and some pointers as to items that you may want to emphasize as you teach the class or small group. This will provide some initial directions that you can use as you teach for 20 minutes.

"Take-Aways"

I've used this term for years, and I always need to explain it! A 'take away' is three or four concepts, truths or ideas that, as those in your class or small group are going through each chapter, they would 'take away' in their minds' or hearts' knowing and understanding. I find it is helpful to know the objective of each lesson and what we want them to learn and remember before starting the lesson.

Additional Questions You Can Ask

As I am sure you've seen, each chapter has eight questions for each participant to have answered prior to coming to the class or small group. Four of these questions are designed for them to ponder during a time of self-reflection. The final four questions are for discussion within the group. You may find that the discussion around these four questions takes up your whole time, or if you choose, feel free to use all eight questions as a part of your group discussion itinerary. Even though four of the questions are designed for self-reflection, hopefully people will be willing to discuss what God showed them through their reflection process. In this Leader's Guide, you will find additional questions to ask if you want more material to discuss.

Scripture Memory Verses

As you will read in the book, I have been a longtime proponent of the spiritual discipline of Scripture memorization. Dallas Willard, former Professor of Philosophy at the University of Southern California and prolific author on spiritual growth wrote, "Bible memorization is absolutely fundamental to spiritual formation. If I had to choose between all the disciplines of the spiritual life, I would choose Bible memorization, because it is a fundamental way of filling our minds with what it needs. This book of the law shall not depart out of your mouth. That's where you need it! How does it get in your mouth? Memorization."[1]

As you lead this study, I strongly recommend that you encourage them to memorize the two verses every week that you can give them to memorize! It really is just a great 'add on' to your lesson and will help them as they learn the truths found in God's word found in each chapter.

Here are a couple of keys to Bible memorization: First, teaching your people to memorize each passage in a particular way is an important and helpful tool. As I have memorized scripture verses, I always memorize the title first, then the reference, then the verse, then I say the reference again.

Here is an example:

> Filled with Love For Others (title)
> John 13:34-35 (reference)
> "A new commandment I give to you, that you love one another: just as I have loved you, you also are to love one another. By this all people will know that you are my disciples, if you have love for one another." (the Bible verse)
> John 13:34-35 (repeat the reference again)

If you and your participants say each of these parts in this order, you will find it helpful because not only will you memorize the verse, but the title acts as the 'handle' that will help you retrieve the verse that you've memorized when you need to recall it. For the Scripture verses recommended for memorization for this study, just use the name of the Mark of a Disciple that corresponds with the verse. (Use the example above for a reference.)

The final step for successful Scripture memorization is having a 'Scripture Memory Buddy' to both help keep you accountable and to quiz you on the verses as you memorize them. This could be a spouse, friend or accountability partner. Having someone in your life whom you know is going to ask you to repeat them from memory is very helpful!

---

1. "Spiritual Formation in Christ for the Whole Life and Whole Person" in *Vocatio*, Vol. 12, no. 2, Spring, 2001, p. 7

There are a couple of apps for smartphones that are very helpful in memorizing Scripture. The one I like is called *Bible Memory: Remember Me*. While 'back in the day' we would write our Scripture memory verses on cards and have a hard holder that would keep our cards organized, now with apps like Remember Me, you can memorize them in several different ways, and can move them from 'new' to 'due' to 'known' and as you are memorizing the verses, the app will help you memorize them several different ways. There is even a web interface that you can enter the verses from a PC or Mac, and they sync automatically with the app. It can be found on the Apple or Android app stores.

Action Steps

For each chapter, I'll provide Action Steps that you can challenge your small group or class with in order to see and experience growth in each of the Six Marks of a disciple of Jesus. Again, I would highly recommend that you leave 10 minutes or so to talk about this as a group. I have included questions like:

- 'What areas do we each want to work on as a result of this chapter?'
- "How is God working in your life as a result of what you've read and what areas do you want to be held accountable?'

Finally, please know that I'm praying for you as you lead your group. In writing this book and trying to help you lead your group well, my heart's desire is to see Christians grow into dedicated disciples of Jesus. I hope and pray that your small group or class will benefit greatly from the time spent in this book and in God's word together!

Leader's Guide:

Chapter 1

Opening Paragraph

In setting the stage for the book, I have tried to give the reader an understanding of the difference between a Christian and a disciple of Jesus. Whatever you can to do to facilitate this discussion will be helpful. The purpose is to start well and to set the stage for the rest of the book. I am pretty sure that many of your participants have not thought much about the difference between the two terms, and as we see throughout the New Testament, Jesus wants us to become His fully devoted followers.

Take-Aways

Chapter 1 includes only a couple of take-aways. First, if you are a Christian, you should want to become a disciple of Jesus. Second, as you'll see throughout this chapter, being a devoted disciple of Jesus takes work and time and effort, and the outcome is worth it! Emphasize that our best life is lived as we seek deep communion with Him, and God's glory is revealed as we grow to be more like Jesus.

Additional Questions You Can Ask

Let's talk more about the difference between a Christian and a disciple of Jesus.
1. The author mentions Paul's admonition in Philippians 2 that we must "work out your own salvation with fear and trembling, for it is God who works in you, both to will and to work for his good pleasure.' How does that concept strike you?

Action Steps

A few action steps that you could recommend for your people to work on over the next week:
1. We will determine to do our best to learn what it means to be a disciple of Jesus and take whatever steps necessary to accomplish this task.
2. We will determine to learn the Scripture memory verses and memorize them.

Scripture Memory Verses
Mark 1:17
2 Corinthians 13:5

Leader's Guide:

Chapter 2

Opening Paragraph

As we start with the first of the Marks of a Disciple of Jesus, we start with a big one: *A disciple of Jesus has fully identified with Jesus and will openly admit that he or she belongs to Christ.* This chapter begins to develop what will become a theme for the book: Jesus wants us as His disciples to renounce all for Him.

You may be familiar with Campus Crusade's (now called *"Cru"*) way of sharing the Gospel: the Four Spiritual Laws. In this tool, at the end of the presentation they ask if I am on "the throne" of control of my life, or if Jesus is. This question of who is on the throne is an important one for this chapter! As we really understand what Jesus has done for us, what that finished work on the Cross means in terms of our identity, and how we can then live out our lives fully sold-out for Him, we learn what it means to be fully identified as a disciple of Jesus.

Take-Aways

1. Jesus really has cancelled the record to debt in our lives. Help your people know that and live in that truth daily.
2. Jesus does not want us to continue to battle thoughts of self-doubt and loathing. Through Christ, we have victory!

3. Romans 1:16 is attainable for us all!

Additional Questions You Can Ask
1. In what ways can Romans 1:16 become a 'life verse' for us all?
2. Although this is one of the eight questions at the end of the chapter, go deeper with 'What are the biggest obstacles to fully identifying with Christ?'

Action Steps
1. In what areas can we help each other 'renounce all' for Christ?
2. Who in the group needs accountability as they surrender all and fully identify with Christ?
3. We will continue to determine the importance of Scripture memory and time in God's Word in being a disciple of Jesus. In what ways will we ensure that we are holding each other to the values we have said are important?

Scripture Memory Verses
Romans 1:16
Philippians 3:7-9

Leader's Guide:

Chapter 3

Opening Paragraph

To say that a disciple of Jesus has a supreme love for Jesus should not be a revolutionary concept, but in our battle with our own sin, it is true that placing Jesus in the #1 spot of our lives takes deliberate effort. The three 'First Steps' I've given in this chapter could take up most of your discussion time with your group. Determining who Jesus is (liar, lunatic, or Lord), recalling what He has done in each of our lives, and then rearranging our priorities to reflect the determinations we've made are great first strides toward having a supreme love for Jesus. My prayer is that you and your group have a great discussion around these three topics!

Take-Aways

1. Love the Lord more than you love anything else.
2. Our love for Jesus should be incorruptible and selfless
3. At times, it takes some work on our part to determine who Jesus is and resolve to love Him with everything we have.

Additional Questions You Can Ask

In addition to the eight questions included at the end of this chapter, which will probably take up most of your time, I encourage you to take whatever additional time you may have to focus on the list of statements in this chapter (I admire Jesus, I enjoy His ways, I want His approval, etc.) and drill down with your participants on how many of these are true and what would need to happen for all of them to be true in their individual lives.

<u>Action Steps</u>
1. We want to make strides in the area of priorities and making Jesus the #1 priority in our lives. Let's talk about what ways we need to do that.
2. The goal is to have a love for Jesus that is incorruptible! How can we help each other have this kind of love for Jesus?

<u>Scripture Memory Verses</u>
    Matthew 22:37-40
    Galatians 2:20

Leader's Guide:

Chapter 4

Opening Paragraph

In this chapter, I hope to make a case for the Bible: that it is worth our time to read, to study and to obey. Far too many of us treat the Bible as a book to peruse from time to time. In reality, it is the very Word of God! If we want to know Him, the Bible is the primary means for us to do so. Some of the participants in your group may not have settled the matter of the Bible being the inspired Word of God with 100% certainty. Much of your conversation can be directed in this area as you walk through the points I have made show that the Bible is reliable and that is stands all the tests that you could throw at it to determine its reliability.

The second part of this study then moves on to focus upon 'Once we know it is the Word of God, we then must determine to be reading and studying it daily.' I will be praying for you and your group on this point, for I don't know anyone who is growing in their walk with the Lord who isn't spending time daily in God's Word. It is so important!

You may want to suggest group participation in a Bible reading plan. It may be the energy of 'Hey we're doing this together!' that lights a spark for many in your group. And as leader, don't be afraid to begin asking people in your group questions like, 'So Billy, what have you been learning from God's Word lately?' every time you see them. Doing so will emphasize that while there are a lot of things that you could talk to them about (and you may also want to talk to them about other things!), what they are learning from their time in the Bible is most important!

Take-Aways
1. The Bible passes all the tests of reliability for us to know it is the very Word of God.
2. No one progresses well in their relationship with Jesus without investing time in the Bible on a very regular basis.
3. One of the best ways to get to know God's Word well is to read and study it with others. Move your study of the Bible to near the top of your 'To Do' List.

Additional Questions You Can Ask

Any additional questions you may want to ask could be directed toward helping people solve their issues with the Bible's reliability and helping them find a time and plan to read God's word daily.

Action Steps
1. How do we help each other in accountability to spend time daily in God's word?
2. Can we determine as a group to always counsel each other biblically? In other words, if the Bible is God's Word, can we make a commitment to counsel each other from God's Word before we turn to other sources for counsel?
3. In Joshua 1:8, we read that the 'shall not depart from your mouth, but you shall meditate on it day and night, so that you may be careful to do according to all that is written in it. For then you will make your way prosperous, and then you will have good success.' Can we determine to (1) become a person who is meditating on God's Word constantly, and (2) help each other grow as disciples of Jesus by encouraging each other in meditating on God's Word consistently? This would include Scripture memorization.

Scripture Memory Verse
2 Timothy 3:16-17
Joshua 1:8

Leader's Guide:

Chapter 5

Opening Paragraph

This is one of my favorite chapters in the book, because there may not be a clearer Mark of a Disciple of Jesus than being fruitful for Christ. Jesus' admonition in Matthew 7 is clear: 'every healthy tree bears good fruit, but the diseased tree bears bad fruit. A healthy tree cannot bear bad fruit, nor can a diseased tree bear good fruit. Every tree that does not bear good fruit is cut down and thrown into the fire. Thus you will recognize them by their fruits.'

A common experience in growing in the Marks of a Disciple is that if one does not think they are bearing much fruit in their relationship with God, they can feel inadequate. Be sure to emphasize rather than feeling inadequate, a Christ-follower can use this Mark as a way to see where a person might be in their relationship with Jesus. It's kind of like the 'Which came first, the chicken or the egg' discussion! We read in John 15 that as we abide in Christ, fruit will come, so in this case, we know which came first. As we abide and remain close to Christ, we bear fruit. So,f we don't bear fruit, we can discern what needs to happen with greater regularity! You can frame your group discussion around the First Steps I have provided in the chapter. This will hopefully provide an invigorating discussion with your group!

Take-Aways

1. Just like there is nothing I can do to keep my pear tree from producing pears, fruit *will* come from the disciple of Jesus who is abiding in Him.
2. The first step in bearing spiritual fruit is for us to commit ourselves to abiding in Christ.
3. Idols and unresolved sin in our lives can prevent us from bearing spiritual fruit. Center discussion around surrendering these areas of your lives and commit to helping each other.

Additional Questions You Can Ask

If you have time after going through the eight questions at the end of the chapter, a discussion about spiritual gifts and spiritual gift tests would likely be helpful. Many Christians I talk to about these tests have never taken one, and therefore, may not know how to recognize areas of ministry where they may be able to bear much fruit based on their gifting.

Action Steps

1. How can we as a group help each other to find areas that we may need to surrender to God in order to bear fruit?
2. Can we resolve as a group to be praying for each other in the area of Bearing Fruit?
3. What practices can we develop as a group to help each other abide in Christ daily?

Scripture Memory Verses

Galatians 5:22-23
John 15:4-5

Leader's Guide:

Chapter 6

In my reading and research for this chapter, one of the key thoughts that struck me hardest was that the way we love each other as Christians is reflected in what we say about Christ to the non-Christian world. I believe that if we as Christians can love each other well, with an unconditional, sacrificial love, full of forgiveness and grace, we truly would be the aroma of Christ to those around us.

As I wrote in this chapter, Jesus Himself states that this is one of the ways that people know that we are his disciples: if we love each other well. In leading your participants through this chapter, may I refer you to Peacemakers Ministries and their Peacemakers Pledge. With whatever time you have to teach, making your group familiar with this pledge would be worth your time. On their ministry website, they teach about each of us being 'peacemakers.' From their website, *A peacemaker is a person that has chosen to engage in relational disputes with health and purpose from a Gospel perspective. They seek to work through healthy tension, rather than cause unhealthy conflict between them and others involved. They do this by reflecting on God's Word, listening to others, considering other perspectives, taking responsibility for their actions, and committing to healthy reconciliation between them and the other person.*

Their goals are to deepen the relationship and to grow it through effective communication.[2]

Resolving conflict well is a key to obedience in our commitment to have a deep, sincere love for brothers and sisters in Christ.

Take-Aways

1. The way we love one another in our Christian communities is a reflection of our relationship with Jesus. The outside world is watching!
2. Biblical conflict resolution is both a value and process that we should each keep in the forefront of our minds continually. It is difficult and takes continual work, but the outcome is worth it! We should each always be looking for areas where we may have wronged others and should be quick to get the 'log out of our own eye.' We should also be people who project an openness to being confronted, knowing that in our sinful natures, we will mess up and we want to be quick to ask for forgiveness and seek restoration. Living life together with others with this attitude enables us to obey Jesus' command that we read in John 13, "A new commandment I give to you," Jesus states, "that you love one another: just as I have loved you, you also are to love one another. By this all people will know that you are my disciples, if you have love for one another."[3]

Additional Questions You Can Ask

1. Discuss 1 John 4:20-21: "If anyone says, 'I love God,' and hates his brother, he is a liar; for he who does not love his brother whom he has seen cannot love God whom he has not seen. And this commandment we have from him: whoever loves God must also love his brother." Here are a few key points:
    a. How does it hit us when we read John's words, that if we say we love God but have animosity toward our fellow brother, we're lying about what we say and think about God?
    b. This 'love your brother' is a command given to us by Jesus. What are we saying about our level of obedience to Jesus' commands if we don't work hard at loving each other well?
    c. Just to drill in the point, John says here that we MUST love each other well. 'Must' is a strong word! What does that mean—and what

---

2. https://peacemaker.training/peacemaker/
3. John 13:34-35

does it mean when we don't love each other well?

Action Steps
1. What concrete steps can we take to love each other like Jesus loves us?
2. In what areas are we failing at this? How can we fix it?
3. What individuals do we each have in our church or Christian community with whom we need to walk through a process of Biblical reconciliation?[4]

Scripture Memory Verses
John 13:34-35
Ephesians 4:32

---

4. To find a great summary of the 4-step process of Biblical Conflict Resolution, please visit this webpage: https://rw360.org/the-peacemakers-pledge/

Leader's Guide:

Chapter 7

Opening Paragraph

This is probably the hardest of the Marks of a Disciple that I have written about in the book. We are so sinful and want our own way so deeply that to "deny ourselves and take up our cross daily" is hard. I mess up at this all the time! To fully surrender and have total buy-in to Jesus goes against almost everything we actually want to do! At this stage in the book, you have hopefully covered some ground with the participants in your group and have had some great conversations about what it means to be a disciple of Jesus. I have hoped and prayed that this process would be very beneficial for you, the participants in your group and in the cohesion of the relationships among people in your group. In your discussion of this chapter, you can refer back to the discussions you all have had about determining who Jesus really is, about the value and worth of obedience to Scripture and how you all are working together to love each other well. My deep prayer is that, as a group, you all would determine to help each other deny yourselves and take up your crosses daily, making a group plan to do this well.

Take-Aways

1. As crazy as it sometimes seems, living life as a disciple of Jesus means that our efforts at saving our lives give us no gain. The profit comes when we lose

control. When we give up our desires and our own will for our lives, then we truly see a life best lived coming to fruition!
2. Remember Jesus' own words in Luke 9, "For whoever would save his life will lose it, but whoever loses his life for my sake will save it. For what does it profit a man if he gains the whole world and loses or forfeits himself?"
3. This Mark of a Disciple, together with the others, is best accomplished in our lives when we have others to walk this journey with us and hold us accountable to the things we say we want to do and be in Jesus.

Additional Questions You Can Ask

Although I could provide additional questions, I think that the eight questions I've given you will fill your discussion time. Focus on them and dig deeply into the responses that people give.

Action Steps
1. Identify what is keeping you from giving full control of your life to Christ. As mentioned in the chapter, it may be a spiritual stronghold.
2. How are we as a group going to help each other 'deny ourselves and take up our crosses daily?'
3. Will we resolve to pray often for one another in this pursuit to be a fully surrendered disciple of Jesus? How will we communicate struggles and points needing prayer to each other in this process?

Scripture Memory Verses
Luke 9:23-25
Luke 14:26-27

Leader's Guide:

Chapter 8

<u>Opening Paragraph</u>

This chapter was the hardest for me to write. Although I don't often talk much about spiritual opposition that I may face in my life because it can so easily be overplayed, I definitely felt like the enemy had no intention to allow me to write this chapter. Living our lives as disciples means that we are fully surrendered to Christ—something the enemy is interested in fighting. I pray for you as you go through this chapter with your participants. May God allow breakthrough to happen and, through the blood of Christ, may the spiritual attacks be held back as your people determine to become fully-surrendered disciples of Jesus!

<u>Take-Aways</u>

1. Jesus wants to have the very first place among all our relationships.
2. As mentioned in this chapter, it is not possible to be a disciple of Jesus without committing yourself to Jesus exclusively and unconditionally.
3. Having a biblical community and church leaders committed to making disciples goes a long way to having a church full of disciples of Jesus!

Additional Questions You Can Ask
1. What is keeping you from fully surrendering your life to Jesus?
2. What steps do you need to take to become a disciple of Jesus?
3. How has this study helped you become a disciple of Jesus?

Action Steps
1. Go back through all of the questions in each of the chapters and make an 'action list' of areas of your life with Christ you want to work on over the next year.
2. If you don't have a accountability partner to help you in this journey, pray that God would give you just the right person.
3. Take this book to your church leadership and ask them to use it to create an environment that creates disciples!

Scripture Memory Verses
Colossians 3:9-10
John 19:25-27

Additional Notes:

Made in the USA
Middletown, DE
31 March 2019